PRAYING WITH
POWER

PRAYING WITH
POWER

LOWELL LUNDSTROM

 *Whitaker House*

Unless otherwise indicated, all Scripture quotations are taken from the *King James Version* (KJV) of the Bible.

PRAYING WITH POWER

Lowell Lundstrom Ministries
East Highway 10
Sisseton, SD 57262

ISBN: 0-88368-470-5
Printed in the United States of America
Copyright © 1981 by Lowell Lundstrom

Whitaker House
580 Pittsburgh Street
Springdale, PA 15144

3 4 5 6 7 8 9 10 11 12 13 14 / 06 05 04 03 02 01 00 99 98 97 96

Contents

Foreword

Airplanes have always amazed me, especially the giant Boeing 747 jets. Each time I fly in one I get excited. I wonder if the huge structure will actually become airborne. When the plane finally lifts off, I feel like standing in the aisle and cheering for the designers and engineers who created such an avionic wonder.

Despite its immense size, pilots have told me the 747 is easy to maneuver. Boeing designers have harnessed the mammoth power of the jet engines so well that the giant aircraft responds to just a few ounces of pressure on the controls.

God is the greatest power in the universe. He sustains a hundred billion galaxies with the precision of the finest watch. In fact, a Russian scientist has discovered that since astronomers began to time the movements of our solar system, the earth's day has only lengthened by 1/600th of a second.

God, our Creator and Father in heaven whom some mistakenly refer to as "the Force" or "the First Cause," has placed His power at your command. The question is this: How do you release His mighty power on your behalf? The answer is that you do it through prayer. The most important thing you can learn to do is pray effectively, with power, and get results. That is what this book is all about.

God says, *"Call unto me, and I will answer thee, and show thee great and mighty things, which thou knowest not."*[1] Just as the pilot guides the giant Boeing 747 with the touch of his hand, God has shown you how to pray and release the power that sustains a hundred billion galaxies.

Isaac Newton, a scientist to whom the world owes a great debt, said, "I can take my telescope and look millions of miles into space; but I can lay my telescope aside, get down on my knees in earnest prayer, and I can see more of heaven and get closer to God than I can when assisted by all the telescopes and material agencies on earth."

Few people realize the riches that are available to them through prayer. Years ago in Russia, an elderly woman was being moved from her home into a state-owned institution for the poor. One of the movers noticed a picture on the piano. Picking up the snapshot, he inquired, "Isn't this a photo of your son, John?"

"Yes," the mother replied. "He has gone to America, and I am left alone."

"But I happen to know that he has done very well for himself," the man said. "Hasn't he ever written to you? Hasn't he sent you any money? He should have taken better care of you than this!"

"Oh, he has written to me," the mother said, "but all he ever sends are little pictures. I suppose they are pictures of his friends, but they look rather old for John."

"You haven't thrown them away, have you?" the man asked.

"Oh no," she replied. "I have saved every one of them, waiting for my boy to come home and tell me who they are. But I guess he isn't coming."

Then she led him into the bedroom to see the pictures her son had sent to her. The bedroom walls were covered with thousands of dollars' worth of five-, ten- and 20-dollar bills. These were the "pictures" she had been talking about. She was rich but didn't realize it.

Paul the Christian Apostle did not want the early believers to make the same mistake. He wrote to them, *"That God...may give unto you the spirit of wisdom and revelation in the knowledge of him: THE EYES OF YOUR UNDERSTANDING BEING ENLIGHTENED; THAT YE MAY KNOW WHAT IS THE HOPE OF HIS CALLING...AND WHAT IS THE EXCEEDING GREATNESS OF HIS POWER TO US-WARD WHO BELIEVE...."*[2]

If you learn how to pray more effectively, you will be in a position to release God's power for your personal needs and the needs of others. The Apostle James said, *"...ye have not, because ye ask not."*[3] Jesus Christ, who prayed more effectively than any man in history, urges you, *"...ask, and ye shall receive, that your joy may be full."*[4]

I am certain the truths of this book will revolutionize your life. *You will learn how to pray more effectively and get results*. If you are anxious to release God's power—read on!

Scripture References

1 *Jeremiah 33:3*   3 *James 4:2*
2 *Ephesians 1:17-19*   4 *John 16:24*

CHAPTER ONE

Why God Wants You to Pray

Houdini was the greatest escape artist in history. He became world-famous by cheating death with his daring feats. Several times he allowed himself to be bound in chains and thrown into the sea, but instead of drowning he would shed his chains and escape.

However, one time Houdini almost didn't make it. The incident happened in a small town in England. Houdini had boasted that he could escape from any jail if he were allowed to walk in wearing his street clothes and work in complete privacy.

The people of this small English town were proud of their specially constructed jail, and to prove it was escapeproof they invited the famous Houdini to try it out.

Houdini arrived in town with much publicity and fanfare. The officials led him (wearing his street clothes) into the jail cell, closed the cell door and went out of the building. He was left alone.

Immediately the master went to work. First he took off his belt and extracted a tough steel shaft that he would use to open the lock. He was able to crack most locks within a few minutes, but this one was difficult.

He worked for 30 minutes, an hour, an hour and a-half. Why wouldn't it open? Houdini was so exasperated that he was sweating hard, and his confidence began to waver. Finally, after two hours, the master was so physically and mentally exhausted that he collapsed and fell against the door.

It swung open!

It had never been locked. The officials had tricked him. The only place the prison door was locked was in Houdini's mind. He couldn't open the door because of his *locked-in* mentality.

This same principle is true of many people today—they are *locked in* to limiting habits and thought patterns so that they are unable to live abundant lives. This is why Jesus said, *"...ye shall know the truth, and the truth shall make you free!"*[1]

Many people are mentally bound when it comes to prayer. Since the beginning of history men have wondered how to approach their Creator. This is why the disciples asked Jesus, *"Teach us to pray!"* (Luke 11:1).

I used to question prayer. I couldn't understand why—if God is all-powerful, all-loving and all-good—it is necessary to pray. Why should you and I have to pray about things that God has already revealed He wants accomplished?

However, one Bible verse answered my questions and revolutionized my life. Jesus said, *"To him that overcometh will I grant to sit with me in my throne, even as I also overcame, and am set down with my Father in his throne."*[2] This verse not only unlocked my mind to the questions I had about prayer, it revealed what God is trying to accomplish in your life and mine.

Let me share my discovery.

Prayer prepares you to reign with God!

Prayer is the means by which you and I overcome the temptations of evil. It is also the means by which we prepare ourselves for our future roles as co-rulers with Jesus Christ. Jesus said that overcomers will be granted positions of leadership upon His throne in glory.

I had never seen this truth before. Jesus Christ had forgiven my sins and I knew I was on my way to heaven, but I did not realize that God is preparing you and me for the throne. Jesus told His disciples, *"...I appoint unto you a kingdom, as my Father hath appointed unto me; that ye may eat and drink at my table in my kingdom, and sit on thrones judging the twelve tribes of Israel."*[3]

The Apostle John saw a vision of our future in heaven. He wrote, *"...I saw thrones, and they sat upon them, and judgment was given unto them...and they lived and reigned with Christ a thousand years."*[4] Can you imagine such an exciting position—ruling with Jesus Christ? With access to all of God's knowledge, resources and time? The Apostle Paul says, *"If we suffer, we shall also reign with him...."*[5] *"Do ye not know that the saints shall judge the world...? Know ye not that we shall judge angels...?"*[6] When you realize that your final destination in eternity is the throne of God, that God is preparing you to be an administrator with Jesus Christ, you will see the importance of prayer.

Prayer prepares you for your position in heaven. Your struggles with spiritual opposition make you wiser and stronger. As you battle the foes of darkness in prayer, you become better equipped for the throne.

Prayer also gives you divine power and authority!

Prayer is God's appointed method for you to take charge of your life. Prayer is the way you win spiritual battles. Jesus told Peter, *"...thou art Peter, and upon this rock* [the rock of Peter's confession that Jesus Christ is the Son of God] *I WILL BUILD MY CHURCH; and the gates of hell shall not prevail against it.*

And I will give unto thee the keys of the kingdom of heaven: and whatsoever thou shalt bind on earth shall be bound in heaven: and whatsoever thou shalt loose on earth shall be loosed in heaven."[7]

As a Christian, you have divine authority to bind and loose the powers that be—through prayer! You must learn how to exercise this God-given power.

Remember, a policeman has authority. However, a thief is under no obligation to stop running away until the officer exercises his authority and yells, "Stop, police!" Your prayer command sets the forces of God into motion. It is not enough to wish something will happen. You need to command it to happen through prayer!

Jesus said, *"…whoseover shall SAY unto this mountain* [the obstacle in your life], *BE THOU REMOVED* [This is your command], *and be thou cast into the sea; and shall not doubt in his heart, but shall believe that those things which he SAITH shall come to pass; he shall have whatsoever he SAITH."*[8] You can take charge over opposing forces through prayer. This is why Jesus said, *"…He that believeth on me, the works that I do shall he do also; and greater works than these shall he do; because I go unto my Father.''*[9]

Jesus Christ is in heaven, and He is praying for you at this very moment. He is your High Priest appearing before God the Father on your behalf. The Bible says, *"...this man* [the Lord Jesus Christ], *because he continueth ever, hath an unchangeable priesthood. WHEREFORE HE IS ABLE ALSO TO SAVE THEM TO THE UTTERMOST THAT COME UNTO GOD BY HIM, SEEING HE EVER LIVETH TO MAKE INTERCESSION FOR THEM."*[10]

Because Jesus is praying for you from the throne of God, you can do His works here on earth. Jesus said, *"...whatsoever ye shall ask in my name, that will I do, that the Father may be glorified in the Son."*[11]

In reality, God has given you a blank check. Whatever God has promised in His Word can be yours if you claim it. If you have not been using your privilege, heaven's treasury of promises are waiting for you. Earnest prayer is the key to releasing them.

Prayer brings growth!

Once you realize that God's great power is released by your prayer command, you will be encouraged to seek Him with all your heart. The discovery of this truth helped me overcome my reluctance to pray.

Recently I have been teaching my son, Lowell Jr., to play guitar. He is struggling with the difficult chords, and the guitar strings bite into his fingers. His hands are soft, and they often ache from the pressure and the strain.

As a father and guitarist I could easily step in and play the song for him, but then he would never learn how to play it himself. In the meantime I am allowing him to struggle because I know this is the only way he will become an accomplished musician. If he continues, someday we may be playing duets on our guitars and composing music together.

Even Jesus learned from His experiences of prayer. The Bible says, *"...in the days of his flesh, when he had offered up prayers and supplications with strong crying and tears unto him that was able to save him from death…though he were a Son, yet learned he obedience by the things which he suffered; and being made perfect, he became the author of eternal salvation unto all them that obey him…."*[12]

God, your Father in heaven, is anxious for you to grow as Jesus grew—in the school of prayer. And, even though your struggle may be difficult, it is the only way you can mature into a strong Christian.

God is willing to help you. In fact, He has given you authority to enter His presence boldly. The Bible says, *"Let us…come boldly unto the throne of grace, that we may obtain mercy, and find grace to help in time of need."*[13] Jesus says, *"Ask, and it shall be given you; seek, and ye shall find; knock, and it shall be opened unto you…."*[14]

Jesus also reminded His disciples who slept when they should have been praying, *"…the spirit indeed is willing, but the flesh is weak."*[15] To grow strong in God, you must conquer your flesh. Learn how to take charge by asking, seeking and knocking until you get an answer! Don't be discouraged by delays. It's the spiritual way to grow up in God.

Prayer can be a transforming experience!

Prayer enabled Jesus to live the greatest life ever lived. Prayer polished the divine Son of God until He shone with all of heaven's glory.

Once Jesus took Peter, James and John to the top of a mountain to pray. He knelt a distance from the disciples and began to pour out His heart to the Father. As He prayed, His physical appearance was transformed. His face began to shine as the sun, and His clothing glistened. Jesus was literally filled with the power of the Holy Spirit until His body glowed with energy. He was transfigured before His disciples.[16]

This is the way prayer should transform your life and mine. Several years ago I heard the Reverend Earl Goodman say that Jesus may have experienced such a transformation many times although it is only recorded in this one instance. Prayer was the secret of His supernatural life.

If you desire a transformation in your life, *it can be yours through prayer*. If you want to see your loved ones set free from evil forces that have taken them captive, if you want to take authority over the devil, *you can through prayer*. If you want to grow strong in the Lord and win spiritual victories so you will be qualified to rule with Jesus Christ upon His throne in glory—*these things can be yours through prayer!*

Remember, the key to a supernatural life of abundance is prayer. In the next chapter I am going to share the secrets of how you can pull down the strongholds of Satan by determined prayer.

In the meantime, you don't have to be locked in by mental misunderstandings about prayer as Houdini was about the jail cell. Prayer prepares you to reign with God. Prayer gives you divine power and authority, and prayer brings growth.

Prayer is your greatest privilege!

Scripture References

1 John 8:32
2 Revelation 3:21
3 Luke 22:29,30
4 Revelation 20:4
5 2 Timothy 2:12
6 1 Corinthians 6:2,3
7 Matthew 16:18,19
8 Mark 11:23
9 John 14:12
10 Hebrews 7:24,25
11 John 14:13
12 Hebrews 5:7-9
13 Hebrews 4:16
14 Matthew 7:7
15 Matthew 26:41
16 See Matthew 17:1-8

CHAPTER TWO

Pulling Down the Devil's Strongholds Through Prayer

As a Christian, you are at war with the devil and all his hellish hosts. However, you have nothing to fear because Jesus says you will win if you carefully follow His instruction to pray.

Jesus assures you, *"...upon this rock I will build my church; and the gates of hell shall not prevail against it."*[1] At this very moment, Satan is trying to destroy you and your loved ones. You can sense that he is busy behind the scenes, working to manipulate, discourage, depress, confuse and tempt you and your family. But Jesus says that the hosts of hell will not prevail against you. The truth is that—with God—you are much stronger than Satan.

The Bible says, *"For the weapons of our warfare are not carnal, but MIGHTY THROUGH GOD TO THE PULLING DOWN OF STRONGHOLDS...."*[2] By now you realize that Satan is trying to establish a stronghold in your life. But your weapons are mighty through God, so you can tear down the hold that Satan has on you and others. Through prayer, you can penetrate the devil's best defenses.

Years ago, when I first read Matthew 16:18 (where Jesus mentions the gates of hell), I thought of the church as a fortress that Satan was attacking and felt I was safe within the church. But one day I realized that it was the other way around. Jesus meant that you and I as Christians have the power and authority to attack the devil's strongholds! We can tear down hell's gates and recover those who have been taken captive. Jesus says, *"...the gates of hell shall not prevail...."* The devil won't be able to defend himself against your attack. *He cannot withstand the power you possess through prayer!*

Remember, it is up to you to take the initiative. As General George Patton used to say, "History favors the aggressor!" Jesus says, "...the kingdom of heaven suffereth vio-lence, and the violent take it by force."[3] Through prayer, you can attack the devil's strong-holds and conquer. You can recover many of your family and friends who are prisoners of Satan. You can set them free!

The Apostle Paul was a missionary who tore down many of the devil's strongholds. He says, "...we wrestle not against flesh and blood, but against principalities, against powers, against the rulers of the darkness of this world, against spiritual wickedness in high places."[4]

If you want to defeat the devil, here are some facts to keep in mind.

Your weapons are MIGHTY THROUGH GOD!

The Living Bible renders 2 Corinthians 10: 3-5 this way: "It is true that I am an ordinary weak human being, but I don't use human plans and methods to win my battles. I use God's mighty weapons, not those made by men, to knock down the devil's strongholds. These weapons can break down every proud argument against God and every wall that can be built to keep men from *finding Him. With these weapons I can capture rebels and bring them back to God....''* What a terrific way to describe the power of prayer! You may feel weak in yourself, but remember that your weapons are MIGHTY THROUGH GOD.

David was only a teen-aged shepherd boy when he went out against the giant, Goliath, who was nine feet tall. However, David's sling and a few stones were more than sufficient to win the victory—because God was on David's side!

If you feel weak, have no fear; *"...God hath chosen the weak things of the world to confound the things which are mighty...."*[5] The key is your authority. The story is told of two small boys who were playing tag on a busy city street. A policeman who directed traffic from a pedestal in the center of an intersection stepped down for a moment to give directions to a motorist.

One of the boys saw that the pedestal was empty, so he jumped onto it and held up his hand. Immediately the traffic screeched to a halt.

Why? The traffic stopped because of his position of authority. Standing on that pedestal, the small boy carried as much authority as the policeman.

You can apply this illustration to your own need. In yourself, you are weak and without authority. However, in Jesus Christ, upon the rock of His righteousness, you can ask anything in Jesus' name and it will be done. The Bible says, "[God] *hath put all things under his [Jesus'] feet, and gave him to be the head over all things to the church, which is his body....*"[6]

Take note of this. If God has put all things under Christ's feet and you as a Christian are part of His body of believers, then all things are under your feet, too. You have all the authority and power you need to tear down strongholds through prayer. Remember to use the name of Jesus when you pray. Jesus says, *"If ye shall ask any thing IN MY NAME, I will do it."*[7]

Jesus Christ has given you the authority and power to command in His name! If you take your stand on the pedestal of God's Word and pray in Jesus' name, you will stop the devil's traffic.

Joining a fellow Christian in prayer will give you more power to bind Satan!

Jesus says, *"...Whatsoever ye shall bind on earth shall be bound in heaven: and whatsoever ye shall loose on earth shall be loosed in heaven. Again I say unto you, That if two of you shall agree on earth as touching any thing that they shall ask, it shall be done for them of my Father which is in heaven. For where two or three are gathered together in my name, there am I in the midst of them."*[8]

Although you have power and authority over Satan, you will increase your effectiveness by joining another Christian in binding the devil. The Bible says that one shall chase a thousand and two put ten thousand to flight.[9] As the Holy Spirit directs you, bind and loose situations.

Remember, you have the authority to take command. When two dedicated Christians meet to tear down strongholds, there is extra power and authority to get the job done.

The Apostle Paul instructed the Christians in Corinth to take authoritative action regarding a young man in the church who was living in immorality with his stepmother. The fellow refused to repent, so Paul said, *"...when ye are gathered together...with the power of our Lord Jesus Christ...deliver such an one unto Satan for the destruction of the flesh, that the spirit may be saved in the day of the Lord Jesus."*[10]

Several years ago, my brother, Larry, and I had to use this power to bind a man who claimed he was part of the Lundstrom ministry. He had spent a few days with our team, but when I found that he was not completely committed, I offered to help him spiritually by sending him to a place where he could study the Bible. I thought it would strengthen his faith in Jesus Christ.

He only studied for a short time and was soon expelled from that group. Then he began to travel throughout the country, wherever the Lundstroms had held meetings, and deceitfully borrowed money and got involved in immoral relationships.

It was a hopeless situation. He was not part of our ministry, so I could not correct him. By the time the Christians suspected his immorality, he had already taken their money and left a bad testimony for Jesus Christ as well as the Lundstrom ministry.

One day, after much prayer, the Lord guided me to 1 Corinthians 5:4,5. Larry and I agreed in prayer that God would give us authority over this satanic conspiracy.

We fasted for three days before we went to see the man. We found him in a town, masquerading as part of our ministry. When we confronted him, he denied it all, but the Christians had told us what he was doing.

We took authority over the situation. We read 1 Corinthians 5:4,5 and explained it to him. Then we prayed that God would bind him and correct him so that he would learn not to hinder the work of God. I'll never forget the look that swept over his face when we prayed. The Holy Spirit dealt with him severely.

That day he disappeared from the area, and we did not see him until ten years later. Then he shared what a nightmarish judgment he had experienced. He has not repented, but neither is he subverting the work of God. The Lord had given my brother, Larry, and me His authority and power to take charge of this seemingly hopeless situation.

In the case of the Corinthian church, the man who was disciplined repented. In his next letter, Paul urged the Christians to forgive him and accept him back into fellowship. [11] So remember, you have authority in Jesus' name and you should not allow the devil to run over you. If you join another believer in prayer, you will receive additional power to bind and loose situations as the Holy Spirit directs you.

Be careful how you rebuke the devil!

Sometime ago I was in the home of a Christian man who was very zealous for the Lord but seemed to delight in making fun of the devil. He understood the authority of the believer, but he carried it too far.

This brother was the chairman for the Gospel rally where our ministry team sang and preached. Many people in the town were won to Jesus Christ.

After the meeting that night, this precious brother was feeling so good about the spiritual victories that he shouted, "Hallelujah!" and said something to this effect: "Lowell, we really kicked the hell out of the devil, didn't we?"

Instantly an alarm went off within my spirit. I smiled and said something courteous in reply, but I went to bed troubled. I knew what he said was wrong, but I didn't know how to explain it to him from God's Word.

Down through the years, I'd heard other Christians make fun of Satan, but I felt it was wrong. I felt that taking command over the devil and making fun of him are two different things. That night I prayed, "Lord, show me what's wrong with this attitude that so many Christians are expressing."

The next morning I picked up my Bible, and my eyes fell on these words in Jude: *"Yet Michael the archangel, when contending with the devil he disputed about the body of Moses, durst not bring against him a railing accusation, but said, The Lord rebuke thee."*[12]

This was the answer I needed. The Bible says that after Moses died the devil tried to possess his body, but Michael—God's chief angel—came down from heaven and argued with the devil about it. In the struggle, Michael was careful about the way he dealt with the devil. Instead of making fun of him, he said, "...*The Lord rebuke thee.*" He did not say, "I rebuke thee"; he left that awesome responsibility with God.

You will find Michael's approach very helpful when pulling down the devil's strongholds. Satan is so sly that even in retreat he will tempt you to become arrogant and proud or to use statements that are beneath your dignity. Remember, the devil is a formidable foe. You can lose the battle by dealing with him in a LIGHTHEARTED way.

Don't ever forget that God's Word and prayer will release the power of God on your behalf. A tiny switch can release the power of a great explosive, and a small prayer will release the power of God on your behalf.

Betty Malz, a well-known author and wife of my associate evangelist, Carl Malz, shared this inspiring testimony with me about the faithfulness of God to answer prayer.

"Big Swede" was a lumber contractor in the woodlands of northern Minnesota. He directed crews of lumberjacks, and the wood they harvested was shipped throughout North America.

"Big Swede" loved his wife, Flo, and nearly worshiped her. He weighed 220 pounds and was a tough man on the job, but when it came to Flo his heart was as soft as a marshmallow. That is—except when he was drinking! And he drank from Friday night through Sunday night nearly every week.

When whiskey controlled him, his personality changed and he became a vicious, raging man with a wild temper. After his drinking binges he would go home and abuse his wife, stamping on her with his heavy boots and pulling hair from her head. Flo lived in constant fear.

After his rampage, "Big Swede" would sober up, and then he would rave and threaten to kill the person who had abused his wife while he was drunk. He never believed that he was the one who had abused his wife! This is why the Bible says, *"Wine is a mocker, strong drink is raging: and whosoever is deceived...is not wise."*[13]

For years, Flo believed "Big Swede's" promises to quit drinking, but then her hope died. One day she began to drink in a desperate effort to cope with the situation.

However, a Christian couple began to intercede in prayer for "Big Swede" and his wife. They began to bind the devil and break down his stronghold. On several occasions they tried to tell "Big Swede" and Flo how Jesus Christ could transform their marriage and make them happy, but the miserable couple had no time for God despite their sufferings.

As the drinking and abuse continued, Flo began to plot her bittersweet revenge. Ten years of beatings had built a mountain of hatred in her heart.

One night "Big Swede" came home drunk. When Flo realized that he had fallen into a drunken stupor on the bed, she poured herself a stiff drink to dull her fear. Then she pulled the top bedsheet over his head and secured it to the bottom sheet by tying the four corners together. With a heavy-duty sewing thread, she sewed the two sheets together so "Big Swede" could not escape.

Then she went out to the woodpile and pulled out a board with a nail in it. (She had kept it for this occasion!) She brought the weapon into the house, packed her suitcases and laid the keys on her luggage. She wanted to make a quick getaway when she was finished.

Taking the board with the nail in it, Flo began to beat "Big Swede" with all the fury she had withheld for so many years. She beat him mercilessly, just as he had kicked her during his drunken rages.

"Big Swede" began to curse and writhe in pain beneath the sheets. With a tongue thickened by drink he threatened to kill her, but she continued to beat him until she saw blood spots on the sheets. Then she poured salt through the holes in the sheets, greatly increasing the pain of his wounds.

Flo knew that the burning pain would soon sober her husband, so she ran to the car and sped away, fleeing for her life.

Her heart pounding, she drove to the home of the Christian couple that had been praying for her. She knocked frantically upon their door, disturbing their prayer time. Within minutes she was telling them the terrible tale of what she had done. Again this Christian couple interceded for God's mercy upon "Big Swede" and Flo.

Flo knew she was safe in their home because it was the last place her husband would look for her. Both she and "Big Swede" had made fun of this Christian couple many times.

Because of their kindness, that Sunday night Flo felt obligated to attend their church. Their home had been a peaceful sanctuary and they had hidden her, perhaps saving her life.

At the close of the sermon the minister said, "If anyone here has a problem, come and kneel at the altar and secretly tell God about it. Nothing is impossible with God! He can fix anything, but you must give Him yourself as well as your problem." Flo stumbled forward and knelt down, begging God to forgive her for the horrible thing she had done to her husband. Then she asked God to forgive "Big Swede" for all the beatings he had given her during the past ten years.

Flo had never prayed before and her prayer was hesitant, but it brought such relief and forgiveness that she sighed, "Oh, it feels so good to be loved, to be forgiven, to be clean! O God, give 'Big Swede' just what You have given me."

Two weeks later, she prayerfully and cautiously made her way home. She arrived several hours before her husband returned from work for the weekend. She made him a thick peach cobbler dessert, and as she prepared it she prayed, "O Lord, cause him to know I love him and that You love him and want to help him."

As she poured his coffee at dinner, she noticed that his eyes were tender with love because she had returned. She silently prayed, "O God, as he drinks this warm coffee, let him feel the warmth of Your love and mine."

The following morning when he went out the door, she went into the bedroom and held his pillow to her bosom and prayed, "O heavenly Father, love 'Big Swede.' Give him peace when his head lies on this pillow tonight. Like a policeman, silently arrest him when he is tempted to drink. Stop him!"

Then Flo went into the living room and sat down in "Big Swede's" chair and prayed,

"O God, when 'Big Swede' sits in this chair this weekend, don't let him drink. Let his body absorb the love I feel for him now and the love You are offering him."

Three weeks later, on a Sunday morning, Flo gathered enough courage to invite "Big Swede" to the little church where she had first prayed. But he replied, "Naw, it don't sound like fun to me!"

At the close of the service the pastor gave the same invitation he had given before. "If you have a need you cannot handle yourself, come and kneel in the presence of Jesus and let Him help you."

This time Flo went forward and knelt for her husband. She wept and begged, "Please, God, do for 'Big Swede' what You did for me." Immediately she heard a voice to her right reply, "Your prayer has been answered." She wondered what was happening—"Am I becoming too religious or overly emotional? Does God reply out loud to people when they talk to Him?"

Turning slowly to the right she saw the 220-pound man trembling and weeping at the altar. "Big Swede" was pleading with the merciful Savior, saying over and over, "O

God, give me what You gave Flo. God, give me what You gave Flo."

On the way home that morning, Flo put her arm around his large shoulders and dared to ask, "'Big Swede,' what made you go to church this morning?"

He replied, "I sat in my chair and turned on the TV and heard a preacher praying. I couldn't stand it, so I turned the TV off. Then I drove to the church. I arrived right after you did since you had to walk.

"I sat in back. When I saw you kneeling up there, I couldn't stand it, Flo. I could stand the beating, but I couldn't stand the praying."

Then Flo said, "Why, 'Big Swede,' you've never heard me pray."

"That's right. I never heard you, but I felt you!"

Scripture References

1 *Matthew 16:18*
2 *2 Corinthians 10:4*
3 *Matthew 11:12*
4 *Ephesians 6:12*
5 *1 Corinthians 1:27*
6 *Ephesians 1:22,23*
7 *John 14:14*

8 *Matthew 18:18-20*
9 *See Deuteronomy 32:30*
10 *1 Corinthians 5:4,5*
11 *See 2 Corinthians 2:1-11*
12 *Jude, verse 9*
13 *Proverbs 20:1*

CHAPTER THREE

The Power of Intercessory Prayer

"**Y**ou ain't nothin' but a hound dog cryin' all the time!"

The year was 1956, and the singer wailing on the radio was not Elvis Presley, but Lowell Lundstrom—a young rock-a-billy entertainer with a dance band from Sisseton, South Dakota.

I was singing on one of my weekly radio shows in northeastern South Dakota. Before my conversion, I owned and managed a country-rock dance band. When I began to visit Connie's Bible-preaching church, the Christians began to pray for my soul. Soon the Lord began to deal with my heart and I began to think of God and eternity.

I am convinced that my wife, Connie, and I were saved because of intercessory prayer. There would not be a Lundstrom ministry today if the Christians in the Sisseton church had not banded together to pray for us.

Connie taught me some country-style Gospel hymns, and I began to incorporate them in the band's radio shows. Before long, these hymns were the only songs I enjoyed singing. "Hound-dog," "Rock Around the Clock" and the other rock 'n' roll and country love ballads felt empty.

I didn't know that the Christians in the Sisseton church were praying for Connie and me. They were calling out our names to God almost continually. When our radio program came on the air, they would turn their radio dials down for the first part of the show (during the noisy rock 'n' roll and bar room songs) and then turn the volume up when Connie and I sang the hymn at the end. Then they would begin praying that God would save me and restore Connie to fellowship with the Lord.

Praise God, their prayers worked! Within a year, Connie and I came to Christ and were wonderfully saved. God's power had been released on our behalf.

Someone has said, "Intercessory prayer is love on its knees." If you love God and lost souls, you will find a time to pray. The prophet Samuel told King Saul, "...*God forbid that I should sin against the Lord in ceasing to pray for you....*"[1] Jesus says, "...*if two of you shall agree on earth as touching any thing that they shall ask, it shall be done for them of my Father which is in heaven.*"[2]

Prayer is a ministry. Just as some serve God by preaching, singing, witnessing or teaching, everyone can serve God through faithful, fervent, intercessory prayer.

An unusual partnership develops between an intercessor and God. Consider this statement carefully: TO A CERTAIN EXTENT, GOD GIVES TO THEM PRAYERFUL CONTROL OF HIMSELF AND BECOMES THEIR WILLING AGENT: and when the time comes when all mysteries are solved and the record of all lives is truthfully revealed, it will probably be seen that not those who astonished the world with their own powers, but those who quietly through prayer used God's power, were the ones who made the world move forward" (E. P. Roe).

When you pray, God gives you a great measure of control over events

God becomes your agent of deliverance. I believe He places His power in your hands to prepare you for your role in His coming Kingdom. Note this verse carefully and prayerfully: *"Thus saith the Lord, the Holy One of Israel...ASK ME OF THINGS to come concerning my sons, and concerning the work of my hands COMMAND YE ME."*[3]

Many Christians do not understand their role as intercessors. One brother said to me, "Lowell, you don't mean to imply that you can manipulate God, do you?" I replied, "No, I cannot manipulate God (because the question implies a selfish motive on the intercessor's part and weakness on God's part). However, you and I, by the authority given to us by God Himself in Jesus Christ, can change God's mind.

One day in 1540, Martin Luther's friend, Frederick Myconius, became deathly ill. He wrote a farewell letter to Luther. When Luther received the letter from his dying friend, he sent back this reply: "I command thee in the name of God to live because I still have need of thee in the work of reforming the church. The Lord will never let me hear that thou art dead, but will permit thee to survive me. For this I am praying. *This is my will, and may my will be done because I seek only to glorify the name of God.*" By the time Luther's letter reached him, Frederick had already lost his ability to speak, but in a short while he was well and strong again. God answered Luther's prayer in its entirety because Frederick outlived Luther by two months!

Moses was one of the greatest intercessors in history

There was a time Moses changed God's mind. The people of Israel had sinned so greatly that God was going to destroy them

all. God told Moses, "...*I have seen this people, and behold, it is a stiffnecked people: now
therefore let me alone, that my wrath may wax
hot against them, and that I may consume
them....*"4 Then Moses pleaded with God,
"...*Turn...and repent of this evil against thy people.*"5 *"And the Lord repented of the evil which
he thought to do unto his people.*"6

When Moses prayed his earnest prayer of
intercession, GOD CHANGED HIS MIND!
Moses commanded God in a very special
way—earnestly desiring the best for God
and His people. Purity of heart and mind is
required of the one to whom God says,
"COMMAND YE ME."

Jesus said, "...*The harvest truly is plenteous,
but the laborers are few; PRAY YE therefore the
Lord of the harvest, that he will send forth laborers into his harvest.*"7 The reason our Lord
urges you to intercede, to ask God the Father
to send forth laborers into the harvest, is that
He has gone into partnership with the
church in saving the world. The tragedy is
that many Christians do not realize that God
is waiting for their command.

God is waiting for you and me to take hold of His promises!

God has given us the keys to the Kingdom. When we pray—God moves! A good illustration of how intercessory prayer works can be found in government. Each state within the United States has laws a governor must enforce. If, for example, a state declares that first-degree murder is punishable by death, the man who is convicted of first-degree murder must die. The law declares it so! However, if hundreds of concerned citizens were persuaded that the condemned man's act of murder was the result of special circumstances (*e.g.*, his wife was cheating on him) and that he was not a killer at heart, they could pass a petition around. If they gathered enough names representing pleas for the guilty man's life, the governor would be justified in taking a second look at the case. If, after reviewing the evidence and considering the petition, the governor decides that the man deserves another chance, he has the authority to grant a full and free pardon. However, you can imagine how difficult it might be for a governor to move mercifully without a petition.

The law of God states, *"...the soul that sinneth, it shall die."*[8] *"For the wages of sin is death...."*[9] So the question arises, How can God enforce His holy law by punishing the sinner and still be merciful to him?

The answer is this: through intercessory prayer. Once when God was searching for a way to save the nation of Judah from destruction, He said, *"...I sought for a man among them, that should make up the hedge, and stand in the gap before me for the land, that I should not destroy it: but I found none. Therefore have I poured out mine indignation upon them; I have consumed them with the fire of my wrath...."*[10] God was looking for an intercessor to plead with Him for the people, a man like Moses who would pray. But he found none.

When General Dwight D. Eisenhower became President of the United States, he chose this prayer text for his inaugural speech: *"If my people, which are called by my name, shall humble themselves, and pray, and seek my face, and turn from their wicked ways;*

then will I hear from heaven, and will forgive their sin, and will heal their land.''[11]

Abraham was an intercessor

You may remember the story of Sodom and Gomorrah. The Bible says a great cry came out of these two homosexually crazed cities. The cry was of the innocent children whose mothers were out chasing women and whose fathers were out chasing men.

God realized that the people had corrupted themselves beyond the possibility of repentance. To mercifully prevent the cancerous spread of the corruption, He had to destroy the cities. However, the Lord had a good friend by the name of Abraham who lived in the vicinity.

According to the account in Genesis 18, God said, *"...Shall I hide from Abraham that thing which I do...?"*[12] In a sentence God said what amounts to this—"Because Abraham and I are partners and friends, it isn't right that I destroy Sodom and Gomorrah without his knowledge." This really amazes me—that you and I can become such close friends of God that He will not move in wrath without first talking it over with us!

When Abraham realized what God was planning to do, he remembered that his nephew, Lot, and his family lived in Sodom. So Abraham began to intercede for the people. He said, *"...Wilt thou also destroy the righteous with the wicked? Peradventure there be fifty righteous within the city: wilt thou also destroy and not spare the place for the fifty righteous that are therein? That be far from thee to do after this manner, to slay the righteous with the wicked... Shall not the Judge of all the earth do right? And the Lord said, If I find in Sodom fifty righteous... then I will spare all the place for their sakes."*[13]

Abraham had to lower his total to 45 righteous, then 40, then 30, then 20 and finally ten. When he sensed that God had reached the bottom line of mercy, he broke off the bargain. *"And the Lord went his way...and Abraham returned unto his place."*[14]

Abraham had negotiated a tremendous mercy pact, just as God had desired. If Abraham had not interceded, Lot and his family might not have been saved. If the fire had fallen without the biblical record that there weren't even ten righteous people within the cities, to this day people would have felt God's judgment was unfair. Now no one can criticize God and be justified.

Just think—if God was willing to spare Sodom and Gomorrah for as few as ten because of intercessory prayer, God will spare our nation if we intercede as Abraham did!

I mentioned Moses a little earlier in this chapter. There was a time when God's patience with the Israelites had reached the limit. God was determined to wipe them out and start over again. But Moses knew God so well that he bargained with Him just as Abraham did. Moses said, *"...Lord, why doth thy wrath wax hot against thy people, which thou hast brought forth out of the land of Egypt with great power, and with a mighty hand? Wherefore should the Egyptians speak, and say, For mischief did he bring them out, to slay them in the mountains, and to consume them from the face of the earth? Turn from thy fierce wrath, and repent of this evil against thy people.*

"Remember Abraham, Isaac, and Israel, thy servants, to whom thou swearest by thine own self, and saidst unto them, I will multiply your seed [children] as the stars of heaven, and all this

land that I have spoken of will I give unto your seed, and they shall inherit it for ever.

"AND THE LORD REPENTED OF THE EVIL WHICH HE THOUGHT TO DO UNTO HIS PEOPLE."[15]

Now, please note that God was fully justified in feeling the way He did. The Israelites deserved to be destroyed for their rebellion—but the prayers of Moses made the difference!

A little later the people rebelled again, and it appeared that God would not alter His decision to destroy them. Moses interceded, *"Oh, these people have sinned greatly and made gods of gold. Yet now, if You will not forgive their sin, blot my name out of the Book of Life!"*[16] Moses had such compassion for the people that he laid his own eternal soul on the line.

No wonder his prayer saved the entire nation of Israel! He wanted nothing for himself but everything for God and His people.

Someone has said that intercession is a humble ministry because only God knows how much of a person's life has been given in prayer. Today, many compete for the chance to play the piano, sing or testify in church. Few compete for the position of intercessor, for the intercessor is alone with God. People don't know what they are missing. In holy conversation with God, high in the throne room of heaven, the intercessor can hear the rustle of angels' wings and see the face of God.

The story is told of several Salvation Army officers who wrote to General William Booth, "How can we win the lost?" His reply was, "Try tears." David writes, *"The sacrifices of God are a broken spirit; a broken and contrite heart, O God, thou wilt not despise."*[17]

A heart truly moved by compassion will express itself in tears.

When Dr. Bacchus of Hamilton College was dying, his doctor came into the room and gave him a brief examination. Then the doctor conferred quietly and seriously with friends standing in the doorway.

"What did the doctor say?" asked Dr. Bacchus.

"He said, sir, that you cannot live more than one-half hour."

"Then take me out of bed and place me on my knees!" he pleaded. "Let me spend the time in prayer for this sinful world." Moments later, Dr. Bacchus passed from bended knee to Paradise.

Scripture References

1 *1 Samuel 12:23*
2 *Matthew 18:19*
3 *Isaiah 45:11*
4 *Exodus 32:9,10*
5 *Exodus 32:12*
6 *Exodus 32:14*
7 *Matthew 9:37,38*
8 *Ezekiel 18:4*
9 *Romans 6:23*
10 *Ezekiel 22:30,31*
11 *2 Chronicles 7:14*
12 *Genesis 18:17*
13 *Genesis 18:23-26*
14 *Genesis 18:33*
15 *Exodus 32:11-14*
16 *Exodus 32:31,32,*
     author's paraphrase
17 *Psalm 51:17*

CHAPTER FOUR

Prayers That Changed History

For the first time in the history of the world the events shaking our planet threaten to annihilate mankind. The end is so near that the Club of Rome, an elite group of scientists and leading statesmen from many countries, has set the doomsday clock to four minutes before midnight.

The Scripture declares, "...*in the last days perilous times shall come.*"[1] Consider the multiple crises the world is facing today.

- THE WORLD IS FACING AN ENERGY CRISIS. We are rapidly exhausting our oil reserves.
- THE WORLD IS FACING A FOOD AND FIBER CRISIS. We are running out

of productive farmland and our great forests will soon be gone.

- THE WORLD IS FACING AN ECO-LOGICAL CRISIS. We have polluted this planet to the point of no return. Our oceans are dying.
- THE WORLD IS FACING A POPULA-TION CRISIS. The poorer nations are not restraining their birth rates, and millions are dying from starvation.
- THE WORLD IS FACING A POLITICAL CRISIS. Ungodly ideologies are winning multitudes. Do you realize that out of the 154 nations in the UN only 13 are considered true democracies? These are Australia, Belgium, Canada, Denmark, Great Britain, the Netherlands, New Zealand, Norway, Sweden, the United States, Israel, Italy and West Germany. The last three have been democracies only since the late 1940s.
- THE WORLD IS FACING A MILITARY CRISIS. Today the nations are rushing for weapons in an endless arms race that costs more than $1 billion a day! With gigantic H-bombs (equaling 15 tons of TNT

for every person on this planet) waiting to be detonated, the question is not Will the world blow up? but When?

With doomsday dead ahead, many have a right to fear. Jesus said the time is coming when wars and destruction will be so terrible that unless God shortens the days there won't be any survivors.[2]

If the world ever needed intercessors, it needs them today! We need to support our leaders with prayer. The Apostle Paul says, *"I exhort therefore, that, first of all, supplications, PRAYERS, INTERCESSIONS, and giving of thanks, be made for all men; for kings, and for all that are in authority; that we may lead a quiet and peaceable life in all godliness and honesty. For this is good and acceptable in the sight of God our Savior."*[3]

You and I are encouraged to pray for the leaders of government. God would never give us this directive unless our prayers made a difference.

Through intercessory prayer, you can direct the course of history!

In 1933, Adolph Hitler rose to power and nearly conquered the world. Can you imagine what would have happened if he had succeeded? This devil-directed führer sent six million innocent Jews to the gas chambers. What would have happened to the other minorities of every religion, race, creed and culture if Hitler had won World War II?

From a military viewpoint, Hitler's great blunder was his decision to attack Soviet Russia instead of England. This mistake destroyed him. Instead of winning the war, his soldiers, tanks and armored divisions became snowbound in one of the worst winters in Russian history. Millions of Christians throughout the world were praying that Hitler would be defeated, and God destroyed the Third Reich's armies with a snowstorm!

There were other times when prayer defeated Hitler's plans. The Battle of Dunkirk is an example. Hitler sent his panzer divisions into France, blitzing the country. British, French and Belgian soldiers fled toward the English Channel after failing to hold the Nazis back.

Hitler could have slaughtered the Allied soldiers within a matter of days. They were trapped. If they tried to escape across the Channel in ships, Hitler's submarines or his Luftwaffe would sink them at sea. The Allied nations considered every possible alternative, and only one remained—God. In desperation, they consulted the omniscient Ruler of the universe.

King George III decreed a day of intercessory prayer throughout the British Empire. Millions of Christians united to pray to God on behalf of the British Army. God answered immediately. On the German side, the Lord sent such a violent storm that every plane was grounded. Tanks bogged down in the mud, and the Germans were held captive by the elements.

On the British side, the sea was as smooth as glass. The weather could not have been better. The English people, comprehending God's awesome miracle, began to send out thousands of small boats. A dense fog aided rescue operations on the French-German side of the Channel. Within hours, 330,000 Allied soldiers were plucked from Hitler's hands. On the English shore, many of them formed circles of prayer to thank God for deliverance from the enemy. God promises, *"...call upon me in the day of trouble; I will deliver thee, and thou shalt glorify me."*[4]

The miracle of Salerno

Another example of how intercessory prayer altered events in World War II took place in Salerno, Italy. The Allies had gambled to establish a beachhead at Salerno in September 1943. They needed this strategic position in order to build a new front and drive the Germans back.

At the very hour the Allied soldiers were storming the beach at Salerno, Rees Howells, director of a Bible college in Great Britain, met with his students for a regular evening prayer session. The session was divided into two prayer meetings by a short intermission. As the students regathered for prayer at 9:45 p.m., they sensed a heavy spirit in the air. Howells addressed them in a trembling voice: "The Lord has burdened me, between meetings, with the invasion at Salerno. I believe our men are in great danger of losing their hold."

Theirs was no ordinary prayer meeting that night. Prayer was intense and urgent. Howells said later, "The Spirit took hold of us and suddenly broke right through in the prayers, and we found ourselves praising and rejoicing, believing that God had heard and answered. We could not go on praying any longer, so we rose...the Spirit witnessing in our hearts that God had wrought some miraculous intervention in Italy. The victory was so outstanding that I looked at the clock as we rose to sing. It was the stroke of 11:00 p.m."

A few days later, local newspapers ran the headline, "Miracle of Salerno!" A front-line reporter gave his eyewitness account of what had happened. He was with the troops that landed at Salerno, and they were just approaching the city when the Germans counter-attacked. The Nazis rapidly advanced, threatening to decimate the Allied soldiers. Unless a miracle happened, the city would be lost. The British troops could not stop the Germans and establish the beach-head at the same time.

Suddenly the Germans ceased firing and an eerie, deathlike stillness settled in. The reporter said: "We waited in breathless anticipation, but nothing happened. I looked at my watch—it was 11:00 at night. Still we waited, but nothing happened; and nothing happened all night, but those hours made all the difference to the invasion. By morning, the beachhead was established." The victory came at 11:00 p.m., right on the heels of travailing prayer.

According to Rees Howells, you cannot simply turn intercessory prayer on when you feel like it. *Intercessory prayer is an advanced stage of prayer in which the Spirit summons you before the throne of God.* He says: "If the intercessor is to know identification and agony, he also knows authority. He even causes Him to change His mind." Howells says that when he reached a place of intercession for a need and believed it was God's will, he always had victory.

When it comes to intercessory prayer, there is a temptation to feel that God's great intercessors were spiritual supermen, unlike you and me. However, one of the most powerful men of prayer was Elijah, and the Scriptures make special mention of his "ordinariness": *"Elias* [the Old Testament prophet, Elijah] *was a man subject to like passions as we are...."*[5]

The Bible says, *"...The earnest prayer of a righteous man has great power and wonderful results. Elijah was as completely human as we are, and yet when he prayed earnestly that no rain would fall, none fell for the next three and one half years! Then he prayed again, this time that it would rain, and down it poured and the grass turned green and the gardens began to grow again."*[6]

During the past 23 years of my ministry, I have been privileged to work with many well-known men and women of God. Their names are on the lips of millions because of their exposure through books, cassette tapes, records and television. I have learned one encouraging fact from these servants of the Lord—they are just ordinary people who try harder.

Sometime ago I went fishing with some fellows, and we had a great time laughing and enjoying the great outdoors. After a few hours, one of the guys looked at me and said, "Hey, Lowell, you're just like us!" I laughed and said, "I'm glad you figured that out. I'm just a country boy God called to sing and preach."

Elijah was an ordinary man who prayed earnestly, and he sealed up the heavens for three and a-half years. Because of his determination in prayer, he was able to humble wicked King Ahab and bring a backslidden nation to its knees.

Intercessory prayer has much greater power than you can imagine. Even the weakest become strong through intercessory prayer. This fact was vividly illustrated in the life of a young English woman by the name of Marianne Adlard who lay twisted and distorted from suffering. Because she was an invalid, she was unable to attend church, but she carried a great burden of prayer for God's work.

In 1872, Marianne read about the ministry of the American evangelist, Dwight L. Moody, and began to pray, "O Lord, send this man to our church." Day after day she prayed that same prayer, believing that Moody was God's man to bring revival.

Only God could bring him to England, however, because Marianne had no way of reaching the evangelist.

God answered her prayer. Moody had visited England five years earlier and was making plans to visit again—informally. He didn't plan to preach. However, the pastor of the church Marianne attended invited Moody to preach for him and the invitation was accepted.

When Moody preached in that church, the power of God fell upon the congregation. As the evangelist gave the invitation to those present to dedicate their lives to Jesus Christ, literally hundreds stood to their feet.

Moody was surprised by the unexpectedly large response and thought his invitation was misunderstood. He carefully reiterated the commitment he was asking the people to make and their response was the same. Realizing that God was working in a special way in this church, Moody decided to preach there for ten more days. As a result, hundreds of Christians rededicated their lives to Christ, and 400 people joined the church.

But Moody was curious as to why there had been such a phenomenal response to his preaching. He began to inquire and discovered that God's miracle came about through the bedridden girl, Marianne, who had prayed that God would send him more than four thousand miles to initiate a spiritual awakening in her church.

In 1901, G. Campbell Morgan, another powerful preacher of D. L. Moody's day, went to visit Marianne. When he walked into her room, he saw that she was lying in her bed as always. Marianne asked him to hand her the *Birthday Book*. He did, and turning to February 5, 1872, Marianne pointed to the signature and Bible verse, "D. L. Moody, Psalm 91." She commented, "He wrote that for me when he came to see me in 1872, and I prayed for him every day till he went home to God." She had prayed for the evangelist for 29 years!

Marianne asked her prominent visitor, "Now, will you write your name on your birthday page and let me pray for you until either you or I go home?"

Morgan, the silver-tongued orator who moved so many for Jesus Christ, recalled later, "I shall never forget writing my name in that book. To me the room was full of the *Presence*. I have often thought of that hour in the rush of busy life, in the place of toil and strain, and even yet by God's good grace I know that Marianne Adlard is praying for me. These are the laborers of force in the fields of God. It is the heroes and heroines who are out of sight and who labor in prayer who make it possible for those who are in sight to do their work and win. The force of it, to such as are called upon to exercise the ministry, can never be measured."

Marianne helped empower D. L. Moody and G. Campbell Morgan's sermons so that these men of God shook the world. If you are physically incapacitated, you can have a great prayer ministry for God. Pray for me just as Marianne Adlard prayed for Dwight Moody, and together we can change history!

Scripture References

1 *2 Timothy 3:1*
2 *See Matthew 24:22*
3 *1 Timothy 2:1-3*
4 *Psalm 50:15*
5 *James 5:17.*
   See 1 Kings 17:1
6 *James 5:16-18,*
   The Living Bible

CHAPTER FIVE

How to Put Power in Your Prayers

Did you hear about the little boy who was saying his bedtime prayers? He knelt down by his bed and prayed, "O God, make me a better boy. But don't worry too much about it because I'm having a lot of fun the way I am!"

Another story is told of a fellow who always prayed the same prayer before going to bed. He became so bored with the prayer that he typed it out and tacked it to the wall. Then, each night when he crawled into bed he pointed to the prayer on the wall and said, "God, You can read it just as fast as I can say it."

Many people are like this man—they give up on prayer because of boredom or failure.

The Bible records the time when the Lord's disciples were unable to cast an evil spirit out of a boy. The child's father said to Jesus, *"Lord, have mercy on my son: for he is lunatic, and...ofttimes he falleth into the fire....AND I BROUGHT HIM TO THY DISCIPLES, AND THEY COULD NOT CURE HIM."*[1]

Can you imagine the disciples' frustration as they gathered around the boy who tossed and writhed uncontrollably on the ground? They had prayed and rebuked the devil over and over again, but nothing had happened.

Then Jesus came and *"...rebuked the devil; and he departed out of him: and the child was cured from that very hour."*[2] Afterward, the disciples took Jesus aside and asked, *"...Why could not we cast him* [the evil spirit] *out? And Jesus said unto them, Because of your unbelief."*[3] Jesus reminded them of their need for faith in God. Then He added, *"HOWBEIT, THIS KIND* [OF DEVIL] *GOETH NOT OUT BUT BY PRAYER AND FASTING."*[4]

In difficult cases, you are wise to combine fasting with prayer. Fasting means to deny yourself pleasures and distractions—such as food, drink and sex—in order to concentrate upon God. As an example of this principle, the Apostle Paul instructs married couples, *"...do not refuse these rights [of sexual intimacy] to each other. The only exception to this rule would be the agreement of both husband and wife to refrain from the rights of marriage for a limited time, so that they can give themselves more completely to prayer...."*[5]

The moment you begin to pray about a great need, you enter into conflict with the dark forces of the spirit world. Remember that Paul says, *"...we wrestle not against flesh and blood, but against principalities, against powers, against the rulers of the darkness of this world...."*[6] Fasting will give more power to your prayers. It will help you to be more alert spiritually because your heart, soul and body will be totally focused upon God.

During the days of Queen Esther, in 479 B.C., King Ahasuerus' wicked adviser, Haman, plotted to destroy the Jews. Queen Esther, who was a Jewess, learned of Haman's plan and sent a message to all of her people to fast and pray for three days. This was a great crisis, and Esther wanted to be certain that their prayers had power!

Moses fasted 40 days and nights on Mount Sinai during the time when God gave him the Ten Commandments (Ex. 34:28).

Jesus fasted and prayed 40 days in the wilderness before He began His ministry. Notice verse 1 in Matthew 4: *"Then was Jesus led up by the Spirit into the wilderness to be tempted by the devil."* Before launching into a period of protracted fasting, be sure you are being led by the Holy Spirit. Some people fast because they think it is a good way to diet or to show others how religious they are. These fasts don't win spiritual victories.

Once God led me to fast and pray for three weeks while I was conducting a crusade in El Centro, California. I sang and preached the Gospel every night during the fast. THIS FAST WAS A GREAT EXPERIENCE. God gave me strength to keep up my strenuous preaching despite my lack of nourishment.

As a result of the 21-day fast, several wonderful things happened. God moved into my ministry in a definite way—I believe it was the turning-point in my calling as an evangelist. My spirit became so sensitive to the leading of the Holy Spirit that I was alive to the mind of God. My desire for food and other earthly pleasures vanished. God was present in power throughout that crusade. Many, many people came to receive Jesus Christ as their Savior, and God performed miracles in lives.

There really is power in fasting! John Wesley, the founder of the Methodist movement, refused to ordain a man into the ministry unless he fasted two days a week. There is a reason for the emphasis on this form of self-discipline. Fasting is a constant reminder to your body that your spirit is going to be boss, that your spiritual hunger will prevail over your fleshly desires. Fasting is also a reminder to pray. When you feel hungry, use that sharp hunger pain as an alarm clock to arouse you to pray even more earnestly.

Throughout my ministry, God has led me to add power to my prayers through fasting. In a difficult situation, a three-day fast will add a powerful new dimension to your prayers. (I would add that if there is a possibility that three days without nourishment could threaten your health, you would be wise to check with your doctor to see if a fast would be harmful.)

To the natural man, the skeptic or the cold-hearted Christian, the idea of fasting sounds foolish. However, the Bible reveals that DESIRE IS THE KEY TO POWER WITH GOD!

Isaiah 64:7 really speaks to my heart. The prophet said to God, *"...THERE IS NONE THAT CALLETH UPON THY NAME, THAT STIRRETH UP HIMSELF TO TAKE HOLD OF THEE...."* Everyone was too lazy, too easy-going, too content to just let things slide along as usual. Powerful praying is hard work, and it requires extra effort from those who want to succeed. *However, you will never make this great an effort without a strong desire!*

Jesus said, *"Blessed are they which do hunger and thirst after righteousness: for they shall be filled."* [7] You will be spiritually fulfilled if you hunger and thirst after God—but you can see that *hunger* and *thirst* are words expressing deep desire.

Do you have a deep desire to see your prayers answered? Do you have a deep desire to see your life transformed? Remember, *desire will create determination, and determination will move God on your behalf.*

In the book of 1 Samuel you can read about a woman named Hannah who was childless. She reached the point where she became so determined in prayer for a son that she would not eat and she wept continually. The Bible says that when Hannah went to pray, *"...she was in bitterness of soul, and prayed unto the Lord, and wept sore."* [8]

Did Hannah's deep desire pay off? The Bible says, *"...the Lord remembered her. Wherefore it came to pass...that she bare a son...."* [9] Her son, Samuel, became one of God's greatest prophets. When you really want an answer to your prayers, things are going to happen!

Jabez—the man who wanted more!

One of my favorite scriptural passages is hidden in the genealogies of 1 Chronicles. In the midst of all the names, the writer states, *"...Jabez was more honorable than his brethren.... And Jabez called on the God of Israel, saying, Oh that thou wouldest bless me indeed, and enlarge my coast, and that thine hand might be with me, and that thou wouldest keep me from evil, that it may not grieve me! AND GOD GRANTED HIM THAT WHICH HE REQUESTED.''*[10]

Jabez is an encouragement to me. His ancestors and descendants seem to have had few ambitions; they are briefly recorded as living and dying. *But Jabez wanted more from God.* He prayed that God would bless him and enlarge his coasts (*i.e.,* bless him financially and materially). He also prayed that God would be with him and keep him from evil. God honored each request. The God of Jabez will honor your requests as well—if you want more, if you are determined in prayer.

Jacob holds on and becomes a prince of God!

Another example of desire in determined prayer is found in the life of Jacob. If you read his biography in Genesis, you will discover that he was a dreamer and a schemer who cheated his brother and deceived his father.

When his brother, Esau, threatened to kill him, Jacob fled. However, 20 years later Jacob had to return home with his wives and children. Esau, who had waited all those years for his revenge, was on the way to meet him with an army of 400 men. Jacob was unarmed. This was the crisis of Jacob's life—and the time for his special prayer meeting with God.

Jacob went out that night and knelt and prayed, *"Deliver me, I pray thee* [O God], *from the hand of my brother, from the hand of Esau, FOR I FEAR HIM, lest he come and slay us all, the mothers with the children. But thou didst say, 'I will do you good, and make your descendants as the sand of the sea, which cannot be numbered for multitude.'"*[11] Jacob reminded God of His promise. He literally prayed the promise of God.

Still trusting in his own shrewdness, however, Jacob prepared a lavish gift for Esau. Then he instructed his servants to go ahead of his caravan and present the gift to Esau as a peace offering. The same night, he hurried his two wives, their two maids, his 11 children and all of his belongings across the Jabbok River.

When Jacob finally had a moment to himself, a stranger suddenly appeared in the darkness and began to wrestle with him. Neither opponent prevailed until the amazing stranger sprained Jacob's thigh. But Jacob held on, realizing that he had come face to face with God.

This was Jacob's finest hour. It was the turning-point in his life. *Jacob was determined to die with God because he knew for certain that he would die without Him!* Although he was wounded and hurting, Jacob's desire for God was greater than his pain.

As the dawn approached, the angel of the Lord said, *"...Let me go, for the day breaketh. And he [Jacob] said, I will not let thee go, except thou bless me."*[12]

The angel replied, *"...What is thy name? And he said, Jacob. And he [the angel] said, Thy name shall be called no more Jacob, but Israel: for as a prince hast thou power with God and with men, and hast prevailed."*[13]

Jacob won the contest because he had a deep desire for a miracle from God. That very night God miraculously changed Esau's heart so that he forgave Jacob for all the wrongs he had done. Today when you hear about the nation of Israel in the news, remember that this country is named after Jacob who was transformed when he became desperate for God's blessing.

Some of my happiest moments are spent wrestling with our two sons, Lowell Jr. and Lance (aged 14 and 5). I can easily overpower them, but that is not the point. I want to develop their determination. As a father, it's exciting to feel their little muscles struggling against mine and to see their jaws set with purpose. I want them to become as strong and determined as I am, and more so. I have tried to instill in their minds slogans such as "If it doesn't hurt, you're not doing it right," "The bottom line is blood," "You can't slide uphill" and "History favors the aggressor."

God desires to instill this same principle of determination into your prayer life. HE WANTS YOU TO HANG ON LIKE JACOB. He wants you to be willing to be like Jesus when He sweat blood in prayer. He wants you to become spiritually mature. Jesus taught the principle of tenaciousness in Matthew 11:12—"...*the kingdom of heaven suffer-*

eth violence, AND THE VIOLENT TAKE IT BY FORCE."

When still a young man, the great evangelist, Charles Finney, realized that he needed God's touch on his life. He hiked to a wooded area north of his village, hoping to avoid prying eyes. Finney records, "An overwhelming sense of my wickedness in being ashamed to have a human being see me on my knees before God took such powerful possession of me that I cried at the top of my voice and exclaimed that I would not leave that place if all the men on earth and all the devils surrounded me. I prayed until my mind became so full that, before I was aware of it, I was on my feet and tripping up the ascent toward the road."

He reached home at noon, having prayed in the woods since dawn. Time had become unimportant. He sat down to dinner but realized that he had no appetite. He tried to play hymns on his bass viol but was so moved by God that he could not sing without weeping. He says, "All my feelings seemed to rise and flow out. The utterance of my heart was, 'I want to pour my whole soul to God.' The rising of my soul was so great that I rushed into the room back of the front office to pray. I wept aloud like a child and made such confession as I could with my choked utterance. It seemed to me that I bathed His feet with my tears."

FINNEY DEEPLY DESIRED AN ENCOUNTER WITH GOD and, as a result, he became one of the world's most powerful preachers. His sermons were like those of a gifted attorney pleading for the lives of condemned men. Surveys indicate that 75 percent of his converts remained true until death.

John Wesley and the early Methodists learned how to hang onto God!

In his *Journal*, John Wesley writes about the beginning of the revival that was to shake England and America: "On Monday, January 1, 1739, Mr. Hall, Kinchin, Ingham, Whitefield, Hutchins, and my brother Charles were present in Fetterslane, with about sixty of our brethren. ABOUT THREE

IN THE MORNING [Please note the time!] as we were continuing instant in prayer, the power of God came mightily upon us, insomuch that many cried out for exceeding joy, and many fell to the ground."

John Wesley received such a great outpouring of the Holy Spirit in this meeting that his preaching transformed entire cities. Today, nearly two hundred fifty years later, Methodist churches everywhere witness to the power of God apparent in that man's life.

The Lord is looking for men and women who, like John Wesley, will wait until 3:00 a.m. to see the glory of God. God says, *"Ask of me, and I shall give thee the nations for thine inheritance, and the uttermost parts of the earth for thy possession."* [14]

Never give up!

When it comes to desire in getting something done, a speech of Winston Churchill's is worth remembering. When Churchill became Prime Minister of Great Britain, he was invited to give a speech at the school he attended as a boy. That day the teachers and students assembled and waited expectantly for the great orator to begin.

They would never forget his speech. Churchill stood up and said, "NEVER GIVE UP. NEVER GIVE UP. NEVER, NEVER, NEVER EVER GIVE UP." Then he sat down. That was all he needed to say in order to get his message across.

Apply Winston Churchill's advice to your prayer life —"Never give up. Never give up. Never, never, never ever give up." Remember the Lord's statement: *"...the kingdom of heaven suffereth* [allows] *violence, and the violent take it by force."*[15] If you really want God to answer your prayers, press on! The Kingdom is yours.

Scripture References

1   *Matthew 17:15,16*
2   *Matthew 17:18*
3   *Matthew 17:19,20*
4   *Matthew 17:21*
5   *1 Corinthians 7:5,*
       The Living Bible
6   *Ephesians 6:12*
7   *Matthew 5:6*
8   *1 Samuel 1:10*
9   *1 Samuel 1:19,20*
10 *1 Chronicles 4:9,10*
11 *Genesis 32:11,12,*
       Revised Standard
       Version
12 *Genesis 32:26*
13 *Genesis 32:27,28*
14 *Psalm 2:8*
15 *Matthew 11:12*

CHAPTER SIX

Praying
With
Praise

One of the greatest secrets to answered prayer is learning to pray with praise. Praise is the password to power with God.

The moment you lift your voice in thanksgiving and praise to the Lord, you tune in to the spirit of praise of worshipers gathered around the throne of God in heaven. John the Apostle saw a vision of heaven and wrote, *"...I beheld, and I heard the voice of many angels round about the throne...saying with a loud voice, Worthy is the Lamb [Jesus Christ] that was slain to receive power...."*[1] Then all the worshipers in heaven and earth said, *"...Blessing, honor, and glory, and power, be unto him that sitteth upon the throne, and unto the*

Lamb for ever and ever."[2] HEAVEN RE-SOUNDS WITH THE PRAISES OF GOD.

When you praise God with your whole heart, you are welcoming Him into your life. The Bible says, *"Oh that men would praise the Lord for his goodness, and for his wonderful works to the children of men! And let them sacrifice the sacrifices of thanksgiving...."*[3] The Bible speaks of King David as a man after God's own heart (see 1 Sam. 13:14), and this is what David said: *"I will bless the Lord at all times: his praise shall continually be in my mouth."*[4]

Praise opens heaven's gates to your petition

The Scripture says that God inhabits the praises of His people.[5] Praise will bring your prayers into the presence of God—and when this happens you will get results!

When the early Christian missionaries, Paul and Silas, preached in Philippi, they were taken into custody by the magistrates and beaten. Then they were thrown into the inner chambers of a dungeon. This was a crisis situation, but Paul and Silas knew the power of praise. When they realized they couldn't get out, they praised God in!

At midnight they were singing praises to God when, suddenly, an earthquake shook the prison doors open. Horrified, the prison keeper was about to kill himself, knowing that his life was on the line if the prisoners escaped. *"But Paul cried with a loud voice, saying, Do thyself no harm: for we are all here."*[6] That night the jailer and his whole family received Christ and were baptized.

In the morning the magistrates sent word that Paul and Silas were free to go. *"But Paul said...They have beaten us openly uncondemned, being Romans, and have cast us into prison; and now do they thrust us out privily? nay verily; but let them come themselves and fetch us out."*[7] After the magistrates personally persuaded them to leave the prison, the Apostles visited friends in Philippi and then departed. Through praise in prayer they had seen the miracle of the earthquake and the opened prison doors, they were enabled to reach the jailer and his family for Christ, they were set free with dignity and comforted the Philippian believers.[8]

Bless His
name in all you do

Have you ever wondered how believers worshiped God in centuries past? When archaeologists examined the Dead Sea Scrolls in 1947, they unlocked the story of the Essene believers who lived eight miles south of Jericho in the first and second centuries B.C. and the first century A.D. This is what was found in one of the Scrolls (Column 10 of the *Manual of Discipline*): "As long as I live it shall be a rule engraved on my tongue to bring praise like fruit for an offering.... *I will bless His name in all I do*, before I move hand or foot, whenever I go out or come in, when I sit down and when I rise, even when lying on my couch, I will chant His praise.

"My lips shall praise Him as I sit at the table which is set for all, and before I lift my hand to partake of any nourishment from the delicious fruits of the earth.

"When fear and terror come, and there is only anguish and distress, I will still bless and thank Him for His wondrous deeds, and meditate upon His power, and lean upon His mercies all day long. For I know that in His hand is justice for all that live, and all His works are true. So when trouble comes, or salvation, I praise Him just the same."

Raise your hands heavenward

I have found that making the effort to raise my hands in praise and thanksgiving to God enhances my time of prayer. The raising of hands is a universal sign of surrender; it means, "I give up. I surrender myself to the one before me." When I raise my hands to the Lord, it is an act of surrendering my life to Him.

The Bible says, *"Enter into his gates with thanksgiving, and into his courts with praise: be thankful unto him, and bless his name."*[9] Paul the Apostle wrote to the early Christians, *"I will therefore that men pray everywhere, lifting up holy hands, without wrath and doubting."*[10] The psalmist urges us to praise God: *"...bless ye the Lord.... Lift up your hands in the sanctuary, and bless the Lord."*[11]

When you first raise your hands in praise to God, it may feel strange, but you will find this act of devotion very rewarding. As you praise the Lord, God will come into your praises and you will begin to feel a flow of the Holy Spirit moving through your soul.

Then honor the Lord by saying, "Hallelujah!" (or "Alleluia!"); it means "Praise the Lord!" The Apostle John records in Revelation 19:1, "...*I heard a great voice of many people in heaven, saying, Hallelujah! Salvation, and glory, and honor, and power, unto the Lord, our God....*" The next time you pray, praise the Lord aloud, saying, "Hallelujah!" with your heart, soul and hands raised in worship. You will be joining the heavenly host in a symphony of exaltation!

Praise is your privilege as a believer-priest!

As soon as you become a born-again Christian, you become a believer-priest. The Bible says, "...[He] *that loved us, and washed us from our sins in his own blood...HATH*

MADE US KINGS AND PRIESTS UNTO GOD....''[12]

Your recognition of your own position before God is important. The Lord doesn't want you to go through life with your head down, mumbling, "I'm-just-a-sinner-saved-by-grace." He wants you to hold your head high and raise your hands heavenward. He wants your lips to offer the spiritual sacrifices of praise. The Apostle Peter made this plain: *"...YE ARE A CHOSEN GENERATION, A ROYAL PRIESTHOOD...that ye should show forth the praises of him who hath called you out of darkness into his marvelous light...."*[13]

Our ministry as believer-priests on earth is to be similar to that of Jesus Christ, our High Priest in heaven. The Bible says, *"SEEING THEN THAT WE HAVE A GREAT HIGH PRIEST, THAT IS PASSED INTO THE HEAVENS, JESUS THE SON OF GOD, let us hold fast our profession."*[14] Again the Scriptures say, *"...this man* [Jesus Christ], *because he continueth ever, hath an unchangeable priesthood. Wherefore he is able...to save them to the uttermost that come unto God by him, seeing he ever liveth to make intercession for them."*[15]

As Jesus our High Priest appears before God the Father in heaven on behalf of sinners, you and I as believer-priests are to appear before God here on earth. Our responsibility is also to intercede on sinners' behalf. Praise is the incense we offer God as we approach His throne.

In his day, Job was the greatest man in the Mideast. The Bible says he was "...*perfect and upright, and one that feared God, and shunned evil.*"[16] Job exercised his prayer privilege regularly. When his sons and daughters feasted and held parties, Job "...*rose up early in the morning, and offered burnt offerings according to the number of them all; for Job said, It may be that my sons have sinned, and cursed God in their hearts. Thus did Job continually.*"[17]

He offered sacrifices for each one of his children and prayed priestly intercessory prayers on their behalf—just in case, in the midst of the party, his children may have shown disrespect for God. No wonder God considered Job perfect and upright and said to Satan, "*Hast thou considered my servant, Job, that there is none like him in the earth, a perfect and an upright man, one who feareth God, and shunneth evil?*"[18]

If parents would surround their children with priestly prayers as Job did, they would not have many family problems

The story of Eli also shows the importance of fulfilling your role as a believer-priest in your home. This priest of God failed to discipline his children and intercede for them in prayer. His sons robbed offerings from the Lord and committed fornication.

As a result of Eli's failure as a father, God expelled him from the priesthood. God said, *"...I will judge* [Eli's] *house forever for the iniquity which he knoweth, because his sons made themselves vile, and he restrained them not."*[19] As an appointed priest of God, you are to pray for your family and friends as well as for your nation and the rest of the world. You can sin against God by failing to fulfill your duty as a priest.

A great illustration of the power of praise is found in Exodus 17. The Israelites were leaving Egypt on their way to the promised land of Canaan when they were attacked by Amalekites. The Bible says, *"...now the warriors of Amalek came to fight against the people of Israel.... [And] Moses instructed Joshua to issue a call to arms to the Israelites, to fight the army of Amalek. "'Tomorrow,' Moses told him, 'I will stand at the top of the hill, with the rod of God in my hand!'*

"So Joshua and his men went out to fight the army of Amalek. Meanwhile, Moses, Aaron, and Hur went to the top of the hill. And as long as Moses held up the rod in his hands, Israel was winning; but whenever he rested his arms at his sides, the soldiers of Amalek were winning. Moses' arms finally became too tired to hold up the rod any longer; so Aaron and Hur rolled a stone for him to sit on, and they stood on each side, holding up his hands until sunset. As a result, Joshua and his troops crushed the army of Amalek...."[20]

This story should encourage us to do as Moses did. When he raised his hands in intercessory prayer, the enemy was driven back. As you and I raise our hands in intercession for others, Satan and his forces will also be driven back.

David prayed, *"Hear [O Lord] the voice of my supplications, when I cry unto thee, when I lift up my hands...."*[21] Remember, as a believer-priest you have been given the power and authority to pray for others. IF YOU WANT TO BE WELL RECEIVED BEFORE THE THRONE OF GOD, BEGIN TO PRAY WITH PRAISE AND THANKSGIVING.

Scripture References

1   *Revelation 5:11,12*
2   *Revelation 5:13*
3   *Psalm 107:21,22*
4   *Psalm 34:1*
5   *See Psalm 22:3*
6   *Acts 16:28*
7   *Acts 16:37*
8   *See Acts 16:40*
9   *Psalm 100:4*
10 *1 Timothy 2:8*
11 *Psalm 134:1,2*
12 *Revelation 1:5,6*
13 *1 Peter 2:9*
14 *Hebrews 4:14*
15 *Hebrews 7:24,25*
16 *Job 1:1*
17 *Job 1:5*
18 *Job 1:8*
19 *1 Samuel 3:13*
20 *Exodus 17:8-13,*
    The Living Bible
21 *Psalm 28:2*

CHAPTER SEVEN

The Problem of Unanswered Prayer

Are your prayers hitting the mark? Have you been getting results? Recently a friend of mine told me about the used rifle he had purchased. He couldn't hit a target squarely because the gun barrel was slightly bent and sent the bullet off in the wrong direction. So he discarded the gun.

If your prayers are not successful, there is a reason for your not getting results. Somewhere, somehow, the barrel that guides your prayers has been bent, and I hope this chapter will enable you to straighten it out.

Many people have a very shallow understanding of prayer. They think that praying is like taking a chance on "that great slot machine in the sky." When they put in a prayer, they want to hit the jackpot, and if they don't win they become bitter and cynical. However, God has reasons for answering some prayers and refusing others. Jean Ingelow says, "I have lived to thank God that all of my prayers have NOT been answered."

Some prayers are not answered because God wills differently

God's knowledge of events is so much greater than ours that you and I are wise to trust Him even when He doesn't answer our prayers. One day a little girl prayed for something special. Her daddy asked her if she had received an answer, and she said, "Yes—God said, 'No.'"

One of the best lessons about a *No* answer to prayer is found in the life of the Apostle Paul. He suffered from what he called a "thorn in the flesh." Paul prayed for deliverance from this thorn three times, but God refused to deliver him. The Lord had a specific reason. Paul writes, "*...lest I should be exalted* *above measure through the abundance of the revelations, there was given to me a thorn in the flesh, the messenger of Satan to buffet me, LEST I SHOULD BE EXALTED ABOVE MEASURE. For this thing I besought the Lord thrice, that it might depart from me. And he said unto me, My grace is sufficient for thee: for my strength is made perfect in weakness. MOST GLADLY THEREFORE WILL I GLORY IN MY INFIRMITIES, THAT THE POWER OF CHRIST MAY REST UPON ME.''*[1]

For centuries, Bible students have tried to determine whether Paul's thorn in the flesh was a physical ailment or some other type of irritation. I personally lean toward the idea that his thorn was the Judaizing teachers who followed him everywhere, trying to mislead his converts. But it really doesn't make any difference. The point is that Paul was given many revelations from God and an exalted position in the church, and he could have become proud. God allowed a messenger of Satan to torment Paul in order to prevent that from happening.

God knew that Paul was actually better off with the thorn than without it! After Paul learned God's reason for the thorn, he began to rejoice despite his problem and he continued to grow spiritually. You should do the same. If you have prayed about something and God has said, "No," then rejoice! Give thanks to God because your problem will produce patience in your life, and patience will produce godliness (see Jas. 1:1-4).

However, I caution you to carefully consider all of the facts when applying the example of Paul's thorn to your situation. I have seen many Christians use this incident as a cover-up for their unbelief. Instead of hanging on and praying through on a matter of deliverance, they have given up and used the thorn as a way of escape.

You must have three qualifications before you claim that your thorn is permanent. 1. You must have received many revelations from God. 2. You must have prayed three times for deliverance. 3. You must have heard directly from God that He will not deliver you. This is important—before you give up on prayer for deliverance, you must *clearly hear from God* that He refuses to deliver you.

Some prayers are not answered because you are not ready to receive what you have requested!

When I was a small boy, I begged my father to buy me a big horse. But Dad was wise enough to wait until I grew taller and stronger before he answered my pleadings. God, your Father in heaven, will answer your prayers in His perfect time and according to His perfect plan. But you need to trust and praise Him for the delays.

I have always had a lot of ambition. When I repented of my sins, gave up my entertainment career as a country-rock singer and was called to preach, I launched out with enthusiasm. I wanted to be successful for the Lord.

As a young minister, I attended the large General Council Church Convention of my denomination where thousands of ministers and delegates were gathered. During the convention I found myself praying for an opportunity for my wife, Connie, and me to appear on the program. I prayed, "Lord, please help us to get on the program. If we sing at this convention, many ministers will invite us to conduct crusades in their churches and many more souls will be saved. Please, God, help us *now* because the convention is nearly over."

God did not answer my prayer until 14 years later. Then Connie and I not only had an opportunity to sing, I was also asked to preach to the entire convention crowd of 10,000 who had gathered in Kansas City, Missouri, on that memorable Sunday night. The Lord anointed us in a mighty way. I had fasted and prayed for three days, and my words had great power and conviction. Hundreds responded to the invitation to dedicate their lives to Jesus Christ at the conclusion of my message.

I did not realize until then how foolish my restless prayers, years earlier, had been. As a young minister I was not ready for the responsibility of standing before the convention. God had done me a great favor in delaying His answer to my prayers.

If you have been praying for an opportunity, asking God to open a special door, don't be discouraged if your prayers are not answered right away. You may not be ready to receive the answer. In the meantime, do as Paul did—praise God for whatever problems you are facing. Do your best and serve God where you are.

The Bible says that John the Baptist "...*was in the deserts till the day of his showing unto Israel.*"[2] If you will humble yourself and serve God faithfully in the desert places, in due time God will show you to the multitudes. There is nothing wrong with ambition, but you need to learn patience.

Some prayers are not answered because of wrong motives

The Apostle James says, *"Ye ask, and receive not, because ye ask amiss, that ye may consume it upon your lusts."*[3] Possibly you are asking God for the wrong things. Your prayers may be sincerely misdirected. You may be asking God for the wrong thing for the right purpose or the right thing for the wrong purpose.

The Apostle John declares, *"...if we ask ANY THING ACCORDING TO HIS WILL, he heareth us: and if we know that he hear us...we know that we have the petitions that we desired of him."*[4] The big question is, How can you know what to pray for?

Edwin Robinson said, "The world is...a kind of kindergarten where millions of bewildered infants are trying to spell God with the wrong blocks." If you and I are babes in Christ, immature Christians, we will repeatedly ask God for the wrong things. The Bible says, *"...the natural man receiveth not the things of the Spirit of God: for they are foolishness unto him: neither can he know them, because they are spiritually discerned. BUT HE THAT IS SPIRITUAL JUDGETH ALL THINGS...."*[5]

The only way you can really know the will of God regarding your prayer requests is to read His Word, the Bible, as carefully as you can and to walk in the Spirit. Jesus said, *"IF YE ABIDE IN ME, AND MY WORDS ABIDE IN YOU, YE SHALL ASK WHAT YE WILL, AND IT SHALL BE DONE UNTO YOU."*[6] If you fill your mind with Holy Scripture (*"If...my words abide in you..."*) and fill your heart and soul with the Holy Spirit (*"If ye*

abide in me..."), YOU CAN ASK FOR ANY-
THING AND RECEIVE IT because you are
praying according to God's perfect will.

Some prayers are not answered because of sin

David the psalmist declared, *"If I regard
iniquity in my heart, the Lord will not hear me."*[7]
Several years ago, a Christian man in Cleve-
land, Ohio, backslid and lost his close relationship with God. One day he saw his little
girl fall from a second-story window to the
pavement below. Instantly he cried out to
God. He continued to pray as he ran down
the steps to her side. But his prayers were
unanswered. Afterward he said, weeping,
"I felt nothing. God wasn't there. I was out
of touch."

The Apostle John says, *"...if our heart con-
demn us not, THEN have we confidence toward
God. And whatsoever we ask, we receive of him,
BECAUSE WE KEEP HIS COMMAND-
MENTS, and do those things that are pleasing in
his sight."*[8] James, the brother of our Lord
and head of the early church, says, *"...The*

effectual fervent prayer of a RIGHTEOUS man availeth much."[9] Righteousness (through Jesus Christ) is required of every praying man if he hopes to see his prayers answered. The Lord says, *"I am the vine, ye are the branches, He that abideth in me, and I in him, the same bringeth forth much fruit; for WITHOUT ME YE CAN DO NOTHING."*[10] Stay close to Jesus Christ. Purify your spirit by confessing your sins to Him and desiring that His will be done in your life.

God told His prophet, Ezekiel, *"'Son of dust, these men worship idols in their hearts—should I let them ask me anything?'"*[11] But the strongest words I have ever read about praying in unrighteousness are found in Proverbs 28:9—*"He that turneth away his ear from hearing the law, EVEN HIS PRAYER SHALL BE [AN] ABOMINATION."*

The books of the Old and New Testaments are unanimous in declaring God's pleasure in righteousness and displeasure in sinfulness. Jesus was the most successful Man in history, and He was a Man of prayer, a Man without sin. The reason He received so many answers to prayer is found in John

8:29. He said, *"...I do ALWAYS those things that please him* [God the Father].*"*

This verse is one of the most powerful scriptural bases for the doctrine of sanctification that I have ever found. You can do many things that are not illegal or specifically warned against in the Scriptures. However, the key question is this: Do your actions ALWAYS please God? If not, change your ways. Correct your mistakes. Straighten out your life, and you will begin to see your prayers answered!

A division between you and another believer will hinder your prayers

The Lord cautions that if you know of anyone who has a grudge against you, you should be reconciled before you pray: *"...if thou bring thy gift to the altar, and there rememberest that thy brother hath ought* [anything] *against thee; leave there thy gift before the altar, and go thy way; FIRST BE RECONCILED TO THY BROTHER, AND THEN COME AND OFFER THY GIFT."*[12]

One night when I was just a freshman in Bible college, the Lord taught me the lesson of this scripture. That night I was trying to pray during a prayer meeting, but I didn't think I was getting through to God. Some kind of barrier had been erected between us. (There's nothing worse than trying to pray when you feel that you aren't being heard!)

Then the Lord brought to my mind a conflict that had arisen between another student and me. I'll tell you the background of this situation. The Bible college I attended was very small and the tuition was low, so the school's bank account required careful disbursement of funds. As a result, the cook could not spend much money on meat for our cafeteria meals. We were allowed only a small portion just once a day.

For a meat-eating country boy, this was a great sacrifice. But, for some reason, the sacrifice I had to make seemed more stringent than the other students'. Each night when I went through the cafeteria line, the cook's assistant always seemed to serve the smallest piece of meat to me. Because of what I considered his deliberate discrimination against me, I became bitter.

I didn't think my attitude toward the cook's assistant would affect my relationship with God, but it did. As I knelt there in that prayer meeting, struggling to get my prayer beyond the ceiling of the room, God spoke to my heart: "Lowell, go over to the cook's assistant and ask him to forgive you."

I was shocked, and I prayed silently, "Lord, You've got the wrong man! *He's* the one who should be asking *me* to forgive *him* for discriminating against me. He's the one who's been cheating on the meat!" Despite my protests, the Holy Spirit insisted that I ask this brother for forgiveness.

Feeling unjustly directed, I made my way over to the fellow and said, "I want you to forgive me. For some reason there's something in my personality that offends you. We are just not getting along as well as we should. Please forgive me."

He looked up at me and a bewildered expression swept across his face. He replied, "Lowell, I don't have *anything* against you. I thought you had something against me."

It was my turn to be surprised. I said, "I don't have anything against you except that every time I go through the cafeteria line you give me the smallest piece of meat."

He laughed and said he was sorry, but he was happy to hear I wasn't bearing a grudge against him. Because of my obedience to God that night, this man and I became good friends. Not only that, the barrier between God and me was torn down—and I started getting larger portions of meat.

The next time you approach God in prayer and you sense a barrier, examine your heart and your relationships with others. If the Holy Spirit reminds you of someone who bears a grudge against you or you have bitter feelings that you cannot free yourself from, MEEKLY go to that person and make things right. Be humble, recognizing that your own spirit may be to blame. Then you will find that God will hear your prayers.

Division within your family will also hinder your prayers

It is very easy in these sinful days of high-pressure living to allow quarrels and resentments to rob your family of unity. Someone has said that you cannot dynamite your way through to God if you are harboring a grudge against another.

Specific instructions to husbands

Recently I received a letter from a lady who wrote, "We have family problems that only God can take care of. I'm the only Christian, and sometimes I feel I just can't pray. Jack, my husband, and I are having marital problems, and he drinks."

The Apostle Peter said, *"You husbands must be careful of your wives, being thoughtful of their needs and honoring them as the weaker sex. Remember that you and your wife are partners in receiving God's blessings, and if you don't treat her as you should, YOUR PRAYERS WILL NOT GET READY ANSWERS."* [13]

I can tell you from personal experience that when my wife, Connie, and I have had a disagreement, we have found praying difficult. A willing spirit that is quick to forgive is a key to answered prayer. Jesus says, *"Blessed are the merciful: for they shall obtain mercy."* [14] God's answer to your prayer is an act of mercy, and you can trigger God's mercies by being merciful and forgiving to your mate.

Because the Lord views husbands and wives as one, couples must work to maintain that unity if they are to receive His full blessing. For Connie and me, some of the most meaningful moments in life are when we kneel together and share our prayers and praises to God.

If you feel that your prayers are only half as powerful as they should be, encourage your mate to join you in prayer. Praying together will increase the number of answers you receive.

A withholding spirit will shut heaven to your prayers

The Bible teaches that a giving spirit opens heaven to your prayers. Luke describes Cornelius, who was a very generous man, this way: *"There was a certain man...called Cornelius...a devout man, and one that feared God with all his house, which gave much alms* [gifts] *to the people, and prayed to God alway."*[15]

One day an angel appeared to him and said, *"THY PRAYERS AND THINE ALMS ARE COME UP FOR A MEMORIAL BEFORE GOD."*[16] If you read the entire tenth chapter of Acts, you will see that the prayers and gifts of this godly man resulted in his entire household being saved and brought into the Kingdom of God!

The Lord said, *"Will a man rob God? Yet ye have robbed me. But ye say, Wherein have we robbed thee? In tithes and offerings. Ye are cursed with a curse: for ye have robbed me, even this whole nation."*[17] The citizens of the United States only give three percent of their income to charity. Is it any wonder that growing numbers of people are cursed with debts?

Then God said, *"Bring ye all the tithes into the storehouse, that there may be meat in mine house, and PROVE ME NOW herewith, saith the Lord of hosts IF I WILL NOT OPEN YOU THE WINDOWS OF HEAVEN, and pour you out a blessing, that there shall not be room enough to receive it."*[18]

Giving to God opens the windows of heaven. The opposite of this statement also holds true. If giving generously (ten percent or more of our income) opens the windows of heaven, then withholding our gifts will shut the windows of heaven to our prayers.

The story is told of a Christian man who invited a hobo into his home and prepared a meal for him. The wanderer watched as his host sliced the bread ever so thinly. Before they ate their meal, the Christian bowed his head and began to pray the Lord's Prayer. Before he could say more than two words, his guest interrupted him.

"Wait, mister. If God is our Father, we are brothers. Right?"

"Why, yes," said the Christian.

"All right then, brother. If we are really brothers, how about slicing the bread a little thicker?"

The wanderer's question not only applies to our giving to others, it also applies to our giving to God. If we really believe that God is *"...Our Father which art in heaven...,"*[19] then we need to share thicker slices of the blessings we have received from Him.

Under certain circumstances, a person can actually use every cent of his income on expenses and take every possible deduction on his income tax so that there is not one taxable, titheable dollar remaining. But the Bible says we are to give the firstfruits (the *first* tenth) of our income to the Lord if we want the heavens to open to our prayers. When we honor this biblical instruction, God will pour such a great blessing upon our lives that we won't know how to handle it!

The Bible warns, *"Whoso stoppeth his ears at the cry of the poor, he also shall cry himself, but shall not be heard."*[20] One of the most often memorized verses of the New Testament is 2 Corinthians 9:7—*"...God loveth a cheerful giver."* If you want God to answer your prayers quickly, learn to become a cheerful giver. Give quickly from a grateful heart. Your love for the Lord and His work will open the windows of heaven for you!

Some prayers are not answered immediately because of a great spiritual battle in progress

Someone has said, "Reserve your judgment against God. If time does not set you to

singing, eternity will." When you begin to
pray, more happens than you realize! Satan
tries to block the answers to your prayers.

Few men in history have had the godliness and determination to pray and move
God. Noah, Daniel and Job are three whom
God mentioned to the prophet Ezekiel. The
Lord was so grieved by the sins of His cove-
nant people that He finally said, *"Though
these three men, Noah, Daniel, and Job, were in
it, they should deliver but their own souls by their
righteousness."*[21]

I have always been impressed by the fact
that God mentioned three men who could
change His mind and hold back His righteous wrath! God help you and me to be as
godly and determined in our prayers.

There is a tremendous story in Daniel 10
that provides an insight into the spirit world.
The incident reveals some of the unseen
struggles that take place when you pray.

God had given the prophet Daniel a vision
of things to happen to the Jews in the last
days, and Daniel felt such a great obligation
to interpret this vision that he fasted and
prayed for three weeks. Finally a messenger
from God appeared, and he told Daniel,

"...Fear not...for from the first day that thou didst set thine heart to understand, and to chasten thyself before God, THY WORDS WERE HEARD, and I am come for thy words. BUT THE PRINCE OF THE KINGDOM OF PER-SIA [the angel of darkness that represented Persia] *WITHSTOOD ME ONE AND TWEN-TY DAYS: but lo, Michael, one of the chief prin-ces* [of God's angelic hosts], *came to help me.... Now I am come to make thee understand...."*[22]

Combat with satanic forces hindered God's messenger for 21 days! I find it inter-esting that Satan's emissary is referred to as the "prince of Persia." Today the world is being shaken by satanic spirits at work in the Mideast to thwart God's will. These forces will continue to upset the world until Jesus Christ returns in power and might.

Remember Daniel when you pray. If you feel that your prayers are not getting through to God—or that God's answers are not getting through to you—keep on pray-ing. There's a battle in progress!

The victories won by prayer
By prayer must still be held.
The foe retreats, but only when
By prayer he is compelled.

Scripture References

1 2 Corinthians 12:7-9
2 Luke 1:80
3 James 4:3
4 1 John 5:14,15
5 1 Corinthians 2:14,15
6 John 15:7
7 Psalm 66:18
8 1 John 3:21,22
9 James 5:16
10 John 15:5
11 Ezekiel 14:3,
    The Living Bible
12 Matthew 5:23,24
13 1 Peter 3:7, TLB
    The Living Bible
14 Matthew 5:7
15 Acts 10:1,2
16 Acts 10:4
17 Malachi 3:8,9
18 Malachi 3:10
19 Luke 11:2
20 Proverbs 21:13
21 Ezekiel 14:14
22 Daniel 10:12-14

CHAPTER EIGHT

The Lord's Pattern of Prayer

Did you hear about the Sunday School teacher who was helping her class to memorize the Lord's Prayer? The children kept getting it mixed up. One little boy said, "Our Father who art in heaven, HOWARD be Thy name." Another said, "Lead us not into PENN STATION," and yet another said, "Our Father who art in heaven, HOW'D YOU KNOW MY NAME?"

The Lord's Prayer is so important that Jesus taught it to His disciples twice—once during His Sermon on the Mount[1] and again after a time of personal prayer.[2] Before we rush into the perfect prayer, we should review Jesus' two important lessons about prayer.

1. Most of our praying should be done in private

The Pharisees loved to stand on street corners and piously perform their prayers for bystanders. Jesus says, *"...They have their reward. But thou, when thou prayest, ENTER INTO THY CLOSET, and when thou hast shut thy door, pray to thy Father which is in secret; and thy Father which seeth in secret shall reward thee openly."*[3]

I do not find many people who want to stand on street corners and pray. Because of the antichrist culture that surrounds us, it's hard to get people to pray in public at all. Have you ever noticed how Christians pray the blessing over their meals in restaurants? I call the speedy deliveries "headache specials." A person will quickly bow his head with his hand on his forehead as though he'd just gotten a flash of a migraine, and scarcely a second later he'll be eating.

One minister's teen-aged daughter was ashamed to pray over her meals in the high school cafeteria because she thought the other students would make fun of her. She tried to solve the problem by dropping her fork on the floor. When she stooped under the table to pick it up, she mumbled, "God, bless the food. Amen."

Many Christians have lost their boldness. A few years ago I heard a story about Stuart Hamblen (composer of the song, "It Is No Secret [What God Can Do]"). He was eating in a noisy restaurant with several of his friends, and the diners around them were drinking and cursing. Hamblen was disturbed by their disregard for the Lord. So when the waitress brought in the food, the songwriter stood to his feet and loosed his deep, resonant voice: "O GOD, BLESS THIS FOOD IN JESUS' NAME. AMEN!" People who heard his prayer said that the boisterous diners quieted down instantly.

If we pray in the presence of others, we should pray boldly, in sincerity. But the lesson we can learn from Matthew 6:5,6 is the importance of having a closet of prayer, a place where we can meet God privately. In these sinful times the devil has destroyed nearly all of the prayer closets. All of the surveys I have taken in 23 years of evangelism across the United States and Canada have indicated that not more than one in ten Christians spends as little as ten minutes with God in Bible study and prayer each day. How tragic!

Also, more than seventy-five percent of the Christians we have surveyed are troubled with depression or fits of temper. These surveys have proved to me time and again that communion with God is the key to a happy and fulfilled life. It's as one man shared with me: "Lowell, if I don't read my Bible and pray in the morning, I can't get along with myself—to say nothing of getting along with my wife!"

Do you have a prayer closet? Do you have a place where you meet with God until He strengthens your soul? If Satan has destroyed your prayer closet, make a new one today. Find a place to meditate upon God's Word and pray without distractions and interruptions. Then meet God there at an appointed time each day. If you cannot be there for some reason, find another place to spend time with God.

For many years I have gone on "dates" with God. If there are too many distractions when I need to pray, I get into the car and drive away. (Connie's and my four children are usually busy practicing music, listening to records and tapes, talking or watching TV in the confined space of our bus, so finding a place to be alone with God can be difficult!) Sometimes when I'm parked on a side road, people occasionally drive by and stare. But I don't care. I enjoy being alone with God. Other times I take a walk and talk things over with the Lord.

A friend of mine used to work at a company where many of the employees were ungodly and abusive with their language. When he needed to be alone with God, the only private place for prayer that he could find during a work break was a rarely used elevator. He would stop the elevator between floors and there pour out his soul to God until he was spiritually refreshed.

My wife, Connie, worked as a secretary during my last year of Bible college. The office had 45 secretaries, and Connie could not find one corner in which to be alone with God. So, during lunch break she folded her arms on her desk and put her head down on them. Everyone thought she was resting, but she was actually praying.

I heard of one lady who worked at an outdoor vegetable stand beside the main street of a large city. When she needed to be alone with God, she flipped her apron over her head and prayed silently amid all the pedestrians and traffic.

Jesus said that if you want to be successful in prayer, you must make yourself a prayer closet—the sooner the better!

2. *Jesus taught us not to repeat ourselves in prayer*

True prayer is not measured by the number of our words but by the urgency of our requests. Jesus said, "*...when ye pray, use not vain repetitions, as the heathen do: for they think that they shall be heard for their much speaking. Be not...like...them: for your Father knoweth what things ye have need of, before ye ask him.*"[4]

Years ago, Rowland Hill was the Billy Graham of England. He was a man of prayer and won thousands of people to Jesus Christ. He said, "I like ejaculatory prayer; it reaches heaven before the devil can get a shot at it." I agree. The best prayers are often the sudden ones.

When you pray, you don't need to review the problem for God; He knows your need before you even mention it. Simply begin to thank Him and praise Him for all that He has done for you. Remind Him that His Word promises that He will meet every one of your needs. Then lay claim to His promises. But don't bore God with repetition and review.

Actually, people often pray prayers that sound pretty but don't make common sense. At mealtimes, for instance, many pray, "Lord, bless the hands that prepared this food. Amen." Have you ever examined this prayer? Why pray that God bless only the hands? Wouldn't it be better to pray that God bless the entire person? I know what is meant by this prayer, but that is not what is said. The problem is that we learn little jingles and repeat them, but we aren't really praying. How often do you hear these phrases: "Lord, lead, guide and direct us," "We thank Thee for everything," "Bless the gift and the giver," and "Bless this food to our bodies and us to Thy Service"?

I believe these phrases can be prayed with sincerity—but they are often recited without a second thought. Jesus warned us against using meaningless repetition. Watch out for "weasel words" that have all their meaning sucked out or, after awhile, you'll discover that you are mouthing words that have no meaning to either God or man.

In Luke 11 the disciples came to Jesus and said, *"...Lord, teach us to pray, as John* [the Baptist]*...taught his disciples."*[5] Jesus replied, *"...When ye pray, say, OUR FATHER WHICH ART IN HEAVEN, HALLOWED BE THY NAME. THY KINGDOM COME. THY WILL BE DONE, AS IN HEAVEN, SO IN EARTH. GIVE US DAY BY DAY OUR DAILY BREAD. AND FORGIVE US OUR SINS; FOR WE ALSO FORGIVE EVERY ONE THAT IS IN-DEBTED TO US. AND LEAD US NOT INTO TEMPTATION; BUT DELIVER US FROM EVIL."*[6]

In the Sermon on the Mount, Jesus gave a slightly different version, and since then the popular Lord's Prayer has been stylized a bit more. I believe the version we often recite together is correct, and I will use it from this point to explain the perfect prayer. The Lord's Prayer *is* perfect because Jesus gave it to us as an example of how we should pray. All of our prayers should include the elements found in the Lord's Prayer.

TAKE A MOMENT TO STUDY THE OVERVIEW OF THE LORD'S PRAYER THAT I PREPARED FOR THIS CHAPTER (See pages 126 and 127). YOU MAY WANT TO MEMORIZE IT.

The Lord's Prayer tells us about
GOD————————————————

Our Father
which art in heaven,
Hallowed be Thy name.
Thy Kingdom come.
Thy will be done,
on earth as it is in heaven.

OURSELVES————————————

Give us this day
our daily bread.
Forgive us our trespasses
as we forgive those
who trespass against us.
And lead us not into temptation,
but deliver us from evil.

THE KINGDOM————————————

For Thine is the Kingdom,
and the power,
and the glory
forever. Amen.

Reveals who God is.
Tells us where God dwells.
Shows us how God is to be approached.
Explains what God is building.
Informs us what God wants accomplished.
Unveils how God's will is to be enacted.

Reveals that we should ask only for the present.
Tells us we should first ask for basic things.
Shows that we make mistakes and need forgiveness.
Explains that others make mistakes and need forgiveness, too.
Informs us that our desires can deceive us.
Unveils that God will retrieve us.

Reveals that the universe belongs to God.
Tells us that God has sufficient energy to help us.
Explains our joy in serving Him.
Shows that God's Kingdom is the only thing that will last.

Jesus taught the importance of determination in prayer

Jesus followed this outline of perfect petition with two parables about prayer. His first parable was about a man who needed three loaves of bread at midnight. Jesus said, "...*'Suppose you went to a friend's house at midnight, wanting to borrow three loaves of bread. You would shout up to him, "A friend of mine has just arrived for a visit and I've nothing to give him to eat." He would call down from his bedroom, "Please don't ask me to get up. The door is locked for the night and we are all in bed. I just can't help you this time."*

"'But I'll tell you this—though he won't do it as a friend, if you keep knocking long enough he will get up and give you everything you want—just because of your persistence. And so it is with prayer—keep on asking and you will keep on getting; keep on looking and you will keep on finding; knock and the door will be opened. Everyone who asks, receives, all who seek, find; and the door is opened to everyone who knocks.'''[7]

Determination is the key to successful prayer. Alan Redpath says, "Much of our praying is just asking God to bless some folks that are ill and to keep us plugging along. But prayer is not merely prattle; it is warfare."

Someone has said, "THE LAZY MAN DOES NOT, WILL NOT, CANNOT PRAY, FOR PRAYER DEMANDS ENERGY." John Wesley, the reformer who shook the world, said, "Bear up the hands that hang down— by faith and prayer support the tottering knees. Have you any days of fasting and prayer? Storm the throne of grace and persevere...and mercy will come down." Jesus said, *"...men ought always to pray, and not to faint."*[8] To faint means to give up, to quit. The lesson is plain: TO FAINT IS TO FAIL!

Jesus told another parable that corresponds with the one of the man asking his friend for bread at midnight. This parable is of the widow who sought justice from an unjust judge. Jesus said, *"...There was in a city a judge, which feared not God, neither regarded man:*

"And there was a widow in that city; and she came unto him, saying, Avenge me of mine adversary.

"And he would not [avenge her] *for a while; but afterward he said within himself, Though I fear not God, nor regard man;*

"Yet because this widow troubleth me, I will avenge her, lest by her continual coming she weary me.

"[Jesus] *said* [to His disciples], *HEAR WHAT THE UNJUST JUDGE SAITH. And shall not God avenge his own elect, which cry day and night unto him, though he bear long with them* [delay His answer]?

"I tell you that he will avenge them speedily...."[9]

Jesus reminds us again of the importance of determination. HE WHO WILLS WINS AT PRAYER! George Patton once said, "HISTORY FAVORS THE AGGRESSOR."

Many people ask these questions: "Why do I have to be so determined in prayer? If God is loving, why does He make things difficult?" *The answer is that God has determined not to be directed by prayerful playboys! If you want to get results, you must be determined.* Your commitment to get an answer will not only move God, it will change you from a spiritual weakling into a commando for Jesus Christ!

Trench was right when he said, "Prayer is not overcoming God's reluctance; it is laying hold of His highest willingness." God is more than willing to move on your behalf if you will only be determined to take hold of His promises.

Is there ever a time when we should give up on prayer? The answer is Yes! But that moment is much later than most people think. We usually give up too soon.

King David realized that the moment had arrived when his illegitimate child by Bathsheba died. He had fasted and prayed earnestly, but when the baby died, David went on with his life without holding a grudge against God.

The Bible says, "...*the Lord made Bathsheba's baby deathly sick. David begged him to spare the child, and went without food and lay all night before the Lord on the bare earth. The leaders of the nation pleaded with him to get up and eat with them, but he refused. THEN ON THE SEVENTH DAY, THE BABY DIED. David's aides were afraid to tell him.*

"'He was so broken up about the baby being sick,' they said, 'what will he do to himself when we tell him the child is dead?'

"But when David saw them whispering, he realized what had happened.

"'Is the baby dead?' he asked.

"'Yes,' they replied, 'he is.'

"Then David got up off the ground, washed himself, brushed his hair, changed his clothes, and went into the Tabernacle and worshiped the Lord. [After having prayed for seven days and then having his prayer request denied, David's response was not only commendable, but phenomenal! He worshiped God!] *His aides were amazed.*

"'We don't understand you,' they told him. 'While the baby was still living, you wept and refused to eat; but now that the baby is dead, you have stopped your mourning and are eating again.'

"David replied, 'I fasted and wept while the child was alive, for I said, "Perhaps the Lord will be gracious to me and let the child live." But why should I fast when he is dead? Can I bring him back again? I shall go to him, but he shall not return to me.'

"Then David comforted Bathsheba....."[10]

David fasted and prayed for seven days—while the baby lay on the brink of death—before he reconciled himself to God's decision. He held onto God with determination. This is just one instance in David's life that reveals why God loved him so very much. David was known as a man after God's own heart.

Scripture References

1 See Matthew 6
2 See Luke 11
3 Matthew 6:5,6
4 Matthew 6:7,8
5 Luke 11:1
6 Luke 11:2-4
7 Luke 11:5-10
8 Luke 18:1
9 Luke 18:2-8
10 2 Samuel 12:15-24, The Living Bible

CHAPTER NINE

Praying in the Spirit

Have you ever lost your way in a big city and tried to find an access road onto a large freeway? It is one of the most frustrating experiences of life. You are driving alongside the freeway, and you can see the cars speeding past—but you are bogged down on a slow-moving street because you cannot find the access lane onto the super highway.

You may feel just as frustrated about your prayer life. As you read about famous men and women of God, you may wonder how they ever found the access road onto the "Freeway of Prayer." The answer is that they discovered the route to super prayer by the Holy Spirit. The Bible says, "...*through him* [Jesus Christ] *we…have ACCESS by one Spirit unto the Father."*[1] The Holy Spirit is the access lane onto God's Freeway of Prayer.

If you feel inadequate in prayer, this is exactly the way the Apostles felt. Paul declared, *"…the Spirit…helpeth our infirmities* [or shortcomings]: *FOR WE KNOW NOT WHAT WE SHOULD PRAY FOR AS WE OUGHT…."*[2] Paul felt that he didn't know how to pray effectively. In fact, he said "we," which included the disciples who had walked with Jesus during His ministry on earth. According to Paul, they didn't know how to pray effectively without the Spirit's help.

This should not be a surprise because the Holy Spirit was instrumental in bringing us to Jesus Christ.[3] The Holy Spirit was responsible for our spiritual rebirth,[4] and He enables us to pray. Paul urges us to be *"…praying always with all prayer and supplication IN THE SPIRIT…."*[5]

John Fletcher, a Methodist minister from Switzerland, used to pray, "Oh for that pure baptismal flame. Pray, pray, pray for this! This shall make you of one heart and of one soul. Pray for the gifts of utterance."

The reason why praying in the Spirit is so important is that He is the only one who knows the mind of God. For a moment, imagine what you would say if you were called before Her Majesty the Queen of England or the President of the United States. If you are like me, you don't know the procedures of protocol. However, we face a far higher standard of protocol in the presence of our sovereign God!

The Bible says, *"...he that searcheth the hearts knoweth what is the mind of the Spirit, because HE MAKETH INTERCESSION FOR THE SAINTS ACCORDING TO THE WILL OF GOD."*[6] The original Greek word that is often used for the Holy Spirit is *paraclete*. This term referred to the special court-appointed attorney who would stand by an individual and instruct him when he went on trial for an offense. As he stood before the judge, the paraclete stood beside him, prompted him and told him what to say. Having a competent paraclete was a great comfort to anyone who appeared in court.

Jesus said, *"I tell you the truth; It is expedient for you that I go away: for if I go not away, the Comforter* [the Holy Spirit, our Paraclete] *will not come unto you; but if I depart, I will send him unto you."*[7] The Holy Spirit is a Person, and He knows the mind of God. He will enable you to approach God in exactly the right way.

The Holy Spirit will also strengthen your determination to pray. Jesus said, *"Watch and pray...the spirit indeed is willing, but the flesh is weak."*[8] The disciples slept away one of the most important moments in the life of Jesus Christ. As Jesus agonized in the garden of Gethsemane and sweat drops of blood, His disciples snored. This is what prompted Jesus to say, *"...the spirit...is willing, but the flesh is weak."*

If you are like me, there are times when praying is the very last thing your flesh wants to do. You feel as dead as a stump. This is when you and I need the Holy Spirit to move upon us and give us the desire to pray.

Once when I was preparing our weekly radio broadcast, Connie and I had just gotten home after a long tour of evangelistic meetings. The strain of preaching and long hours on the road had worn our bodies to a frazzle. I worked hard on my sermon and finally had it ready. But when I stood up to deliver it, I felt completely numb. I could not even pray, much less preach a message that would be heard by thousands.

At that moment I cried out to God, explaining my predicament, and I asked the Holy Spirit to quicken me to pray and deliver the message. I'll never forget what happened. Suddenly I felt as though God had turned a heavenly sprinkler on me. I could feel a tingling sensation like ice-cold drops on my back. Soon my entire body was energized. The Holy Spirit swept into my prayer and into my message until I felt His high-voltage power in my words. The experience was fantastic!

The Lord knew that your flesh and mine would fail in prayer unless He sent the Holy Spirit. So, as soon as Jesus was at the Father's right hand in heaven, He made it a matter of utmost importance to send the Spirit. Jesus had commanded His disciples, *"...behold, I send the promise of my Father upon you: but tarry* [wait] *ye in the city of Jerusalem, until ye be endued with POWER FROM ON HIGH."*[9]

Prayer takes power, and Jesus promised to send the necessary power to His waiting disciples. In Acts 1 His instructions are described in greater detail: *"...being assembled together with them,* [Jesus Christ] *commanded them* [the Apostles] *that they should not depart from Jerusalem, but wait for the promise of the Father...."*[10] The Lord said, *"...John truly baptized* [immersed people] *with water; but ye shall be baptized with the Holy Ghost not many days hence."*[11]

Then He said, *"...ye shall receive power, after that the Holy Ghost is come upon you: and ye shall be witnesses* [or, martyrs] *unto me both in Jerusalem, and in all Judea, and in Samaria, and unto the uttermost part of the earth."*[12] So the disciples received power to be Christian martyrs scattered to the ends of the earth. You and I need this same power of the Holy Spirit in order to pray effectively.

If you study the lives of many great praying soulwinners, you will discover that they received great outpourings of the Spirit upon their lives.

Dwight L. Moody was a great success as an evangelist. He drew large crowds to his church, but he says that many of these early victories were accomplished "...largely in the energy of the flesh." The change came when two humble Free Methodist women, Auntie Cook and Mrs. Snow, attended his meetings. They sat in the front row and prayed as he preached. Moody appreciated their intercession so much that he spoke to them about it.

"Yes," they said, "we have been praying for you."

"Why me?" the evangelist inquired, surprised. "Why not the unsaved?" His pride was a bit hurt by the implication that he personally needed prayer.

"Because you need the power of the Spirit," was their answer.

Several weeks later, Moody invited the two ladies to his office to talk more about his need for power.

"You spoke of power for service. I thought I had it," Moody said. "I wish you would tell me what you mean."

Auntie Cook and Mrs. Snow told him all they knew about the infilling of the Holy Spirit. Then they prayed with the pastor and left.

Moody said later, "From that moment, there came a great hunger in my soul. I really felt that I did not want to live if I could not have this power for service." He continued to pray for a special infilling of the Holy Spirit.

Then one day in 1871, the evangelist went to New York on a fundraising mission. As he walked the streets of New York, his soul became hungry for God. Suddenly the Spirit of God swept over him, and his companions could tell something was happening.

One inquired, "Are you sick, Mr. Moody? Shall I call a doctor?"

"No—No!" he replied. "Leave me alone."

"Well, what shall I do?" his friend persisted anxiously.

"Don't do anything. Leave me alone!"

"Well, how can I help?"

"Get me in a room, and get everybody out and leave me by myself!"

Afterward, Moody said that waves of God's power poured over him until he cried out, "Lord, You will have to stop or I will die! I've got all I can hold! God, it is about to kill me!"

From that time on, Moody preached from the same sermon outlines and from the same passages from God's Word. But, instead of just a few responding to his invitation to accept Jesus Christ as Lord, hundreds came forward in every meeting. Moody's ministry was transformed by the Spirit of God.

Charles G. Finney, another of America's great preachers who led hundreds of thousands to Jesus Christ, had a life transforming infilling of the Holy Spirit. After spending time in earnest prayer, he says, "...it seemed as if I met the Lord Jesus Christ face to face. He said nothing but looked at me in such a manner as to break me right down to His feet. I wept aloud like a child and made such confessions as I could with my choked utterance. As I turned and was about to take a seat...I RECEIVED A MIGHTY BAPTISM OF THE HOLY GHOST. NO WORDS CAN EXPRESS THE WONDERFUL LOVE THAT WAS SHED ABROAD IN MY HEART. I WEPT WITH JOY AND LOVE."

Another soulwinner, a preacher of great power, Dr. R. A. Torrey says, "I had been a minister for some years before I came to the place where I saw that I had no right to preach until I was definitely baptized with the Holy Ghost. I went to a business friend of mine and said to him in private, 'I am never going to enter my pulpit again until I have been baptized with the Holy Spirit, and know it, or until God in some way tells me to go.' Then I shut myself up in my study.

"But Sunday did not come before the blessing came.... I recall the exact spot where I was kneeling in prayer in my study...1348 North Adams Street, Chicago. If I had understood the Bible as I do now, there need not have passed any days...."

Samuel Chadwick, a holy minister of the Gospel who wrote a prayer classic entitled *The Path of Prayer*, says, "Early in the year 1882 there came to me an experience that lifted my life to a new plane of understanding and of power. I received the gift of the Holy Spirit.... I had neither power nor might in either service or prayer. I began to pray for power for service, and God led me to the answer by way of equipment for prayer. It was a great surprise to me, for I thought I knew how to pray and had prayed much over the work to which He had sent me. When I began to seek power, my ears were opened before my eyes began to see. I heard testimonies to which I had been deaf. Others had been driven to God, baffled by lack of power, but they always associated the gift of power with an experience of holiness about which I was not keen. *It was power I wanted.* I wanted power that I might succeed, and my chief concern for power was the success it would bring. I wanted success that would fill the chapel, save the people, and bring down the strong fortifications of Satan with a crash. I was young, and I was in a hurry. Twelve of us began to pray in a band, and the answer came....

"HE LED US TO PENTECOST. THE KEY TO ALL MY LIFE IS IN THAT EXPERIENCE. It awakened my mind as well as cleansed my heart. It gave me a new joy and a new power, a new love and a new compassion. It gave me a new Bible and a new message. Above all else, it gave me a new understanding *and a new intimacy in the communion and ministry of prayer; it taught me to pray in the Spirit."*

I trust these testimonies of godly men have touched your heart as much as mine. A great infilling of the Holy Spirit was the key to their prayers and service to God. Praying in the Spirit will help to strengthen and build your life. This is what Jude had in mind when he wrote, *"...ye, beloved, BUILDING UP YOURSELVES ON YOUR MOST HOLY FAITH, PRAYING IN THE HOLY GHOST, keep yourselves in the love of God...."*[13]

Paul the Apostle said, *"...I will pray with the spirit, and I will pray with the understanding also...."*[14] This kind of supernatural expression is the Freeway of Prayer; it will put you in the fast lane to results.

When the Holy Spirit was first poured out upon the early Christians, Peter stood up and said, *"...these are not drunken, as ye suppose* [Many were so filled with God that they looked like men intoxicated by wine]*....But this is that which was spoken by the prophet Joel; And it shall come to pass in the last days, saith God, I will pour out of my Spirit upon all flesh... and on my servants and on my handmaidens I will pour out in those days of my Spirit; and they shall prophesy...."*[15]

Before John the Baptist was born, he was filled with the Holy Spirit.[16] This gave him great power to preach and pray. John looked forward to the time when every believer would experience the fullness of the Holy Spirit. He thundered, *"I indeed baptize you with water unto repentance: but he that cometh after me is mightier than I, whose shoes I am not worthy to bear: he shall baptize you with the Holy Ghost, and with fire...."*[17]

In A.D. 30, the disciples experienced this outpouring of the Holy Spirit and they turned Jerusalem upside down. That very first day about three thousand people repented of their sins and received Jesus as Savior.[18]

This, however, was not the only time the Holy Spirit was poured out. Throughout the time recorded by the book of Acts (over a period of 30 years) believers experienced many outpourings and fillings of the Spirit.

Consider this incident carefully. In Acts 4:31, the disciples were refilled with the Holy Spirit: *"...when they had prayed, the place was shaken where they were assembled together; AND THEY WERE ALL FILLED WITH THE HOLY GHOST, and they spake the word of God with boldness."*

At the moment of conversion, does a person receive all of the Holy Spirit that he can ever get? Not necessarily. Every born-again Christian has the Holy Spirit within, but the baptism of the Holy Spirit is a special filling of the Spirit given to the spiritually hungry. Jesus said, *"If ye then, being evil, know how to give good gifts unto your children: how much more shall your heavenly Father give the Holy Spirit TO THEM THAT ASK HIM?"*[19]

This special filling is a matter of measure. As I have pointed out, every believer has the Holy Spirit, but there is an even greater measure of the Holy Spirit to be received. Jesus said, *"...John baptized with water; but ye shall be baptized with the Holy Ghost not many days hence."*[20]

I would compare the filling of the Holy Spirit at conversion to drinking a glass of water. When you are born again, the Holy Spirit enters your life similar to the way water enters your stomach when you take a drink. However, being filled with the Holy Spirit is more like being thrown into a lake. Then things change—not only is the water on you, you are in the water. It is the same water, but it is in a greater amount.

The Apostles realized that you can be saved and yet need the outpouring of the

Holy Spirit. The Bible says, "...*Philip went down to the city of Samaria, and preached Christ unto them. And the people with one accord gave heed unto those things which Philip spake, hearing and seeing the miracles which he did.*"[21] Then, "...*when they believed Philip preaching the things concerning the kingdom of God, and the name of Jesus Christ, THEY WERE BAPTIZED, both men and women.*"[22]

Here was a group of baptized believers. They were truly converted and, with the exception of Simon the sorcerer, they were ready to become members of the church. However, the Bible says, "...*when the apostles which were at Jerusalem heard that Samaria had received the word of God, they sent unto them Peter and John: who, when they were come down, PRAYED FOR THEM, THAT THEY MIGHT RECEIVE THE HOLY GHOST....*"[23]

Now, if you receive all you need of the Holy Spirit when you are born again—as were the Samaritan Christians—why were Peter and John sent to pray for them to receive the Holy Ghost? The answer is plain: THEY NEEDED TO RECEIVE MORE OF THE HOLY SPIRIT!

Saul, who became the Apostle Paul, was converted on the road to Damascus (A.D. 31 or 32). But Ananias was sent to him so that he would be healed AND FILLED WITH THE HOLY GHOST. The Bible says, *"...Ananias went his way, and entered into the house; and putting his hands on him said, Brother Saul, the Lord, even Jesus, that appeared unto thee in the way as thou camest, hath sent me, that thou mightest receive thy sight, AND BE FILLED WITH THE HOLY GHOST."*[24]

A few years later (between A.D. 35 and 40), Peter went down to the house of Cornelius, the gentile centurion. There Peter preached and *"...the Holy Ghost fell on all them which heard the word."*[25]

Between A.D. 54 and 57, Paul went to Ephesus and asked some of the believers, *"...Have ye received the Holy Ghost since ye believed? And they said unto him, We have not so much as heard whether there be any Holy Ghost."*[26] If you receive all there is to be received when you are born again, why did Paul ask the Ephesian Christians, *"...Have ye received the Holy Ghost SINCE ye believed?"*

Paul discovered that these people were disciples of John the Baptist and that they had been baptized *"...Unto John's baptism."*[27] So Paul preached the Gospel of Jesus Christ to them. *"When they heard this, they were baptized in the name of the Lord Jesus."*[28] You can be sure that the Holy Spirit was within these believers at this moment of baptism. But after their baptism in water, Paul laid his hands on them and *"...the Holy Ghost came on them...."*[29]

I experienced a special outpouring of the Holy Spirit upon my life approximately a week after my conversion. (You'll find the account of my experience in the chapter, "My First Prayers.") This special baptism of the Holy Spirit has been my source of strength for praying and preaching ever since.

Some people may feel they can get along without this special relationship with the Holy Spirit, but I don't. It has been the crankshaft of power that has driven this soulwinning ministry forward since 1957. Through the Holy Spirit, Jesus Christ has become the greatest reality in my life. I thank God the Holy Spirit has given me power to preach so that literally tens of thousands of people have come to a personal saving knowledge of Jesus Christ.

In many ways, you and I are like gliders. We don't have power within ourselves, but if we can find a spiritual thermal updraft, we can be lifted up by its upward movement. The Holy Spirit is moving all over the world today. If you are hungry for a greater dimension of the Spirit in your life, reach out to God.

Jesus said to ASK!
SEEK!
KNOCK!

and the Holy Spirit will be given to you in a greater measure![30]

Scripture References

1 *Ephesians 2:18*
2 *Romans 8:26*
3 *See Romans 8:14-17*
4 *See John 3:5,6*
5 *Ephesians 6:18*
6 *Romans 8:27*
7 *John 16:7*
8 *Matthew 26:41*
9 *Luke 24:49*
10 *Acts 1:4*
11 *Acts 1:5*
12 *Acts 1:8*
13 *Jude, verses 20,21*
14 *1 Corinthians 14:15*
15 *Acts 2:15-18*
16 *Luke 1:15*
17 *Matthew 3:11*
18 *See Acts 2:41*
19 *Luke 11:13*
20 *Acts 1:5*
21 *Acts 8:5,6*
22 *Acts 8:12*
23 *Acts 8:14,15*
24 *Acts 9:17*
25 *Acts 10:44*
26 *Acts 19:2*
27 *Acts 19:3*
28 *Acts 19:5*
29 *Acts 19:6*
30 *Luke 11:9-13*

CHAPTER TEN

Praying Prayers That Penetrate Heaven

When Alexander the Great was 20 years of age, his father, King Philip II, was assassinated. Alexander ascended to the throne of Macedon in 336 B.C. and promptly set out to conquer the world with 35,000 soldiers and an empty treasury. His first goal was the vast Persian Empire.

However, young Alexander was superstitious and wanted a prophecy from the priestess at Delphi before carrying out his ambitions. When Alexander arrived at the heathen temple of Apollos, the temple priests warned him that the public was forbidden entry on that particular day. But he brushed the priests aside, seized the prophetess by the hand and commanded, "Prophesy unto me what I shall be!"

The historian, Plutarch, records, "As if conquered by his violence, she said, 'My son, THOU ART INVINCIBLE!'

"'That is all the answer I desire,' Alexander replied."

Alexander believed her prophecy and by the time of his death in 323 B.C., 13 years later, had conquered most of the ancient world.

Two points stand out in this account: *first*, ALEXANDER'S BOLDNESS TO ENTER THE TEMPLE OF APOLLOS; *second*, HIS FAITH IN THE PRIESTESS' PROPHECY. These are two areas in which Christians need to excel today. Many churches are dying because of weak, ineffectual prayers.

You need to be bold!

The Scripture says, *"LET US...COME BOLDLY UNTO THE THRONE OF GRACE, that we may obtain mercy, and find grace to help in time of need."*[1]

You need to have faith in God's Word!

The Apostle Paul exulted, *"...in...all things we are more than conquerers through him that loved us."*[2]

The question arises, How can you approach the throne of God with boldness? You are only one of many people who are praying. After all, there are more than four billion people in the world today! How can you expect *your* prayers to penetrate heaven? The key to the answer is understanding your position of privilege in Jesus Christ. You will lift a world of problems from your shoulders when you learn to pray with the leverage of God's promises.

Smith Wigglesworth was a man of prayer. God used him to perform so many miracles that he was called an apostle of faith. Wigglesworth was once summoned to pray for a young mother who was possessed by an evil spirit. She raged like a maniac and could not even recognize her husband and baby.

Wigglesworth says, "That brought me to a place of compassion for the woman. Something had to be done, no matter what it was. *Then with my faith I began to penetrate the heavens*, and I was soon out of that house, I will tell you, for I never saw a man get anything from God who prayed on the earth.

"IF YOU WILL GET ANYTHING FROM GOD, YOU WILL HAVE TO PRAY INTO HEAVEN; FOR IT IS ALL THERE. If you are living in the earth realm and expect things from heaven, they will never come. And as I saw, in the presence of God, the limitations of my faith, there came another faith that took the promise, a faith that believed God's Word. And from that presence, I came back again to earth, but not the same man. God gave a faith that could shake hell and everything else.

"I said to the evil spirit, 'Come out of her, in the name of Jesus!' And she rolled over and fell asleep and wakened in 14 hours perfectly sane and perfectly whole."

Praying prayers that penetrate heaven is a key to releasing the power of God on your behalf. Charles Spurgeon says, "God does not hear us because of the length of our prayer, but because of the sincerity of it. Prayer is not to be measured by the yard, nor weighed by the pound. IT IS THE MIGHT AND FORCE OF IT—THE TRUTH AND REALITY OF IT—THE ENERGY AND THE INTENSITY OF IT." If you are going to pray with power and get results, if you are going to go before God with boldness, if you are going to penetrate heaven, YOU MUST KNOW YOUR LEGAL RIGHTS BEFORE GOD.

You have been given the authority to pray in Jesus' name!

Years ago, the Holy Spirit inspired me to write a song with these words:

> *Why should God answer*
> *a sinful man's prayer?*
> *Why should He listen,*
> *why should He care?*
> *The answer is simple,*
> *the answer is plain,*
> *I PRAY IN JESUS' NAME.*
> *Jesus is God's holy Son,*
> *Jesus is the Holy One.*

> *I'm nothing at all,*
> *but He hears me the same.*
> *I PRAY IN JESUS' NAME.*

Jesus taught His disciples, *"...in that day ye shall ask me nothing.* [In other words, we are not to pray *to Jesus,* but pray to the Father *in Jesus' name.*] *Verily, verily, I say unto you, Whatsoever ye shall ask the Father in my name, he will give it you. Hitherto have ye asked nothing in my name: ask, and ye shall receive, that your joy may be full."*[3] So, if you want to have success in penetrating heaven, PRAY IN JESUS' NAME. Your joy will be full. Jesus has given you the assurance that your prayers prayed in His name are heard by the Father.

R. A. Torrey, the famous Bible teacher and associate of D. L. Moody, tells a moving story that illustrates the use of Jesus' name. Torrey says that during the Civil War a father and mother living in Ohio had an only son whom they loved dearly. Not long after the war broke out, he told his parents that he had enlisted in the army and would soon be leaving home. The parents were saddened by the news, but they loved their country and bore the burden of his departure with honor.

After the son left home for the front lines, he wrote home regularly and shared many of his exciting experiences with his parents. His letters were always full of encouragement. Then one day the letters stopped. Many days passed and still there was no news. Soon his parents began to fear the worst.

Finally a letter bearing the insignia of the United States Government arrived. It told of a great battle in which many men had been killed, and their son was numbered among the dead. The parents mourned for days and weeks. The years passed slowly, and the war finally came to an end. Only fading memories lingered.

Then a strange thing happened. One morning as the parents were sitting at the breakfast table, a maid brought word that a poor, ragged man was at the door. He wanted to speak to the man of the house. When she had tried to turn him away, he had handed her a note.

Immediately recognizing his son's handwriting on the note, the father gently unfolded the crumpled sheet and read, "Dear Dad and Mom, I have been shot and have only a short time to live, and I am writing you this last farewell. As I write, there is kneeling beside me my best friend in the company, and when the war is over he will bring you this note, and when he does be kind to him for Charley's sake. Signed, your son, Charles."

Evangelist Torrey concludes the story: "There was nothing in that house too good for that poor tramp...and there is nothing in heaven or on earth too good, or too great for you and me in Jesus' name."

The name of Jesus is the most powerful name in the universe. "...*God...hath highly exalted him, and given him a name which is above every name: that at the name of Jesus every knee should bow, of things in heaven, and things in earth, and things under the earth; and that every tongue should confess that Jesus Christ is Lord, to the glory of God the Father.*"[4] The final fulfillment of this scripture is to come in the future; however, God has exalted Jesus so that at this very moment in heaven requests prayed in His name receive an immediate hearing.

You have been given the power to penetrate heaven in the name of Jesus Christ! This is why you can enter God's presence with boldness.

Today the business world operates on credit. If you pay your bills promptly, giant corporations such as Master Card, Bank Americard and American Express will allow you to use their names in conducting business. I've walked into business places in Rome, Italy, Tel Aviv, Israel, Amman, Jordan, and Cairo, Egypt—where I was a total stranger—and conducted business in the name of Master Card (or Master Charge, as it was once called).

Do you realize that God has granted you the privilege to do business in heaven and on earth in the name of Jesus? This is *your* privilege as a child of God.

I have also noticed that when a purchase price amounts to more than $50, the clerk will phone long distance to have my card and credit verified. A similar thing happens when you pray in Jesus' name. If you try to use His name when your life is not cleansed of sin, you may run into trouble. This is what happened to the sons of Sceva, as recorded in Acts 19. They had been watching Paul and the Apostles cast out evil spirits in Jesus' name, so they tried their hand with the demons.

The Bible says, *"...certain of the vagabond Jews, exorcists, took upon them to call over them which had evil spirits the name of the Lord Jesus, saying, We adjure you by Jesus whom Paul preacheth. And there were seven sons of one Sceva, a Jew, and chief of the priests, which did so.*

"And the evil spirit answered and said, Jesus I know, and Paul I know; but who are ye? And the man in whom the evil spirit was leaped on them, and overcame them and prevailed against them, so that they fled out of that house naked and wounded."[5]

What a sight that must have been! When the demon checked to see if these men had any right to use the name of Jesus and discovered that they didn't, he leaped on them and tore off their clothing. They fled for their lives!

Remember, you have the privilege as a born-again child of God to use the name of Jesus. His name gives you an instant audience with God. Jesus says, *"If ye shall ask ANYTHING in my name, I will do it."*[6]

The name of Jesus also gives you power over Satan. Jesus says, *"Behold, I give unto you power...over all the power of the enemy...."*[7] *"And these signs shall follow them that believe; IN MY NAME shall they cast out devils; they shall speak with new tongues; they shall take up serpents; and if they drink any deadly thing, it shall not hurt them; THEY SHALL LAY HANDS ON THE SICK, AND THEY SHALL RECOVER."*[8]

If you have been trying to penetrate heaven with your prayers, remember to pray to God the Father in Jesus' name. Your prayers in His name will give you power over all the power of the enemy. Learn to use the name of Jesus!

Pray the promises of God!

A. W. Tozer once said, "Too many prayers are no more than monologues on current events. They are suggested by newscasts rather than inspired by the Holy Spirit. They cover the earth like clouds without rain, promising much but delivering little."

God is busy, and if you want to get a hearing in heaven you have to put thought into your prayer requests. God spoke through the prophet, Isaiah, *"Produce your cause saith the Lord; bring forth your strong reasons...."*[9] At another time He said, *"PUT ME IN REMEMBRANCE...declare thou, that thou mayest be justified."*[10] God wants you to remind Him of His promises. He wants you to present His Word to Him as the strongest reason for expecting an answer to your prayers.

Someone has said that there are more than thirty thousand promises of God in the Bible. These promises are your treasure. When you discover what God has pledged to do for you, you will be inspired to ask for miracles. The next time you feel inadequate to handle what seems to be an insurmountable problem, pray this promise: *"I can do all things through Christ which strengtheneth me."*[11] You could also pray, *"...ye are complete in him* [Jesus Christ]*..."*[12] or *"...lo, I am with you alway, even unto the end of the world."*[13]

Here is an example of how you could address God:

Dear heavenly Father, Your holy Word promises that I can do all things through Jesus Christ, that I am complete in Him and that He will always be with me. So, I am claiming Your promises. Help me with this problem. In Jesus' name, amen.

Praying the promises is much better than praying the problem. Prayer often becomes nothing more than worrying out loud. You'll hear people pray like this: "Lord, You know Mr. Smith isn't saved. You know how mean he is to his wife and children. Lord, he drinks and uses Your name in vain." It would be far better to pray, "Father, You have promised, *'Ask of me, and I shall give thee the heathen for thine inheritance....'*[14] I claim Mr. Smith for You. You have promised to give me the heathen, and he's as heathen as any man I know, so I praise You for his salvation. Thank You, heavenly Father, for what You are going to do! In Jesus' name, amen."

When you pray, fill your heart, soul and mind with God's promises. Whatever you do, DON'T REVIEW THE PROBLEMS. Jesus says, *"...your Father knoweth what things ye have need of, before ye ask him."*[15]

A veteran missionary evangelist told me an unforgettable story of an incident in the Orient. A girl whose invalid mother was dying lived near the mission station. On her first visit to a meeting there, she heard the missionary preach God's Word about being converted and born again. She promptly believed God's promise of eternal life and was saved.

The following week she attended the mission service again. This time the missionary's message was devoted to God's promises regarding healing. In the middle of the service, the girl stood up and asked, "Sir, do you mean to tell me that God can heal sick people?" He said, "Yes, God can heal the sick because His Word promises that He will, and He is healing people today."

Then she asked, "Will God heal my mother?" and the missionary assured her that He would. So there, in the midst of the congregation, the girl looked up and prayed, "God, I know You're busy, but I want You to listen to me right now. This man said You would heal my mother. Now, I'll tell You where she lives.

"When You go out of the church, turn right and go two blocks, and then turn right two houses. She lives across the street in the brown house. The front door is unlocked, so go right in. She's in the second bedroom on the left."

Then the girl said to the congregation, "My mother is healed. Let's all go down and see her." The missionary hardly knew what to do, but within moments the excited congregation was following the girl down the street toward her house. When they arrived, her mother was standing in the doorway, shouting, "I'm better! I'm better! I'm better!" The girl's prayer had penetrated heaven because of her childlike faith.

A lady in New Orleans recently told me how she had prayed for some specific needs in her life. She said, "Two years ago I was very dissatisfied with my life, so I made a prayer list of the things I wanted changed.

"First, my husband and I didn't like where we were living and wanted to get into a better house.

"Second, I was embarrassed and ashamed of the old car we were driving. It was unreliable and expensive to maintain.

"Third, we wanted to have a baby—a healthy, happy child we could love and bring up to serve the Lord.

"Fourth, I wanted my husband to have his own business. He is a druggist, and he has some great ideas on how to serve customers and build a business. But we'd never had the capital he needed to try it on his own.

"So I just started praying for these specific needs every day, reminding God of our need. I was careful to pledge that we'd use all these things for His glory and tell everyone we could what God had done for us.

"Well, in just a few months things began to happen. By a series of absolute miracles, God began to answer prayer. It would take too long to tell all the details, but here's where we are today:

"We're living in a beautiful home. (We're the second owners—the past owners had moved out after only a few months!)

"We have a beautiful 6-month-old daughter who is the joy of our lives. I may be prejudiced, but I think she's the sweetest and most beautiful little girl who ever lived.

"I'm driving a 'new' car—a Mercedes! It's not brand-new, but everyone who sees it is amazed by how clean and slick it is. I love it.

"And last—construction is underway right now on my husband's new drug store. It's in a great location, and the man who is financing the project feels it can't help but be a winner!

"So don't tell me prayer doesn't work. I know it does. But you've got to know what you want when you pray. Like the old saying, 'If you don't know where you're going, how will you know when you get there?'"

Dr. Paul Yonggi Cho pastors the largest church in the world—a giant 150,000-member congregation in Seoul, Korea. This outstanding man of God teaches that the Holy Spirit will guide you when you pray the promises of God. He says that there are two Greek words used for the Word of God. The first word is LOGOS, which refers to *the said Word of God* (*i.e.*, God's written Word as you read it from Genesis to Revelation). The second word is RHEMA, which refers to *the saying or spoken Word of God*. In other words, the Holy Spirit will illumine a specific scriptural word or passage to your spirit as you seek God for an answer or help in a specific situation.

As you study the Bible, searching earnestly for an answer from God, a specific LOGOS passage will become RHEMA, the saying Word of God to you. When this happens, you can claim the specific promise in a special way because God has illuminated it to you for your life. The scriptural passage will "jump out" at you. Then you can rejoice because that promise or teaching is God's RHEMA promise to meet your need.

Another way to penetrate heaven is to pray specifically!

Usually, God does not deal with generalities. He is orderly, and He wants you to be specific when you pray. There are many reasons for this. *First*, praying specifically causes you to put your faith on the line and thereby strengthens you. If you pray, "Lord, bless in a wonderful way," you are not being specific enough. Generalities are usually smokescreens to hide behind when you don't want to put your faith to the test. You need to present specific prayer requests.

Second, God has such awesome power that if He were to answer a general prayer request, the result would be earthshaking. You have probably heard someone say that when Jesus raised Lazarus from the dead, He called him by name for a special reason. Unless the Lord had made His prayer specific, *all* of the dead would have risen![16]

On their way to Jerusalem one day, Jesus and His disciples passed through Jericho. They met the blind beggar, Bartimaeus, who *"...sat by the highway side begging. And when he heard that it was Jesus of Nazareth, he began to cry out, and say, Jesus, thou son of David, have mercy on me."*[17]

Several people told Bartimaeus to be quiet. (There are always people who dislike noisy praying.) But Jesus *"...commanded him to be called."*[18] When Bartimaeus was brought to Him, Jesus asked, *"...WHAT WILT THOU THAT I SHOULD DO UNTO THEE? The blind man said unto him, Lord, that I might receive my sight."*[19]

Now, why do you suppose Jesus asked Bartimaeus this question? Wasn't the blind man's need for healing obvious? However, from God's point of view, Bartimaeus had many needs, including cleansing from sin, financial assistance and guidance, to name a few. Bartimaeus was not going to get an answer to his general prayer request, *"...Jesus, thou son of David, have mercy on me."* The Lord wanted something more specific.

When the blind man finally cried out, *"...Lord, that I might receive my sight,"* he was healed. The Bible says, *"...immediately he received his sight, and followed Jesus in the way."*[20]

Many Christians are afraid to present specifics to the Lord. They shrug their shoulders and say, "God, You know more about the situation than I do, so I won't tell You what to do." But this point of view doesn't square with Isaiah 41:21—*"Produce your cause, saith the Lord; bring forth your strong reasons...."* Nor does it account for God's command in Isaiah 45:11—*"...Ask me of things to come...concerning the work of my hands COMMAND YE ME."*

As stated earlier in this book, God is trying to develop you into a Kingdom administrator. He has given you power to bind and loose situations. Jesus says, *"...Whatsoever ye shall bind on earth shall be bound in heaven: and whatsoever ye shall loose on earth shall be loosed in heaven."*[21] What shall be bound or loosed unless you are specific? The expression, "IF it be Thy will," can be a camouflage for doubt.

True, Jesus taught us to pray, *"...Thy will be done...."*[22] *But He did not preface the words with "IF"!* "Thy will be done" honors God and, in many uncertain situations, this expression of submission to God's judgment is in order. But to pray, "IF IT BE THY WILL" allows unbelief to destroy the penetrating power of your prayer. IF is a Trojan horse of doubt dressed up as a gift of humility.

Remember that Jesus Christ has appointed you to be a king, and kings rule. KINGS COMMAND! The Bible says that the Lord *"...hath made us kings and priests unto God...."*[23] If you want to penetrate heaven with your prayers, execute the powers of your holy office.

If you need $152, ask God specifically for $152. Do not pray, "Father, You know my needs." Begin to praise Him for His promises. Pray, "Father, according to Your Word in Philippians 4:19, You have promised to supply all of my needs according to Your riches in glory by Christ Jesus, so I am thanking You in advance for the $152 that I need. In Jesus' name, amen."

Now, in addition to requesting the exact amount, you need to work with God regarding the answer to your prayer. When Peter needed money to pay taxes, Jesus did not hand the money to him. Peter had to go out and catch a fish. He had to cooperate with the Lord.

I know people who have used prayer as a lazy way to get their needs met. They want everything handed to them on a silver platter, the answers to their prayers served to their specifications, without lifting a hand to help.

I like what a Catholic priest said as two fighters entered the ring. One of the fighters crossed himself, and a man sitting next to the priest asked, "Father, will that help?" The priest responded, "It will if he can fight!"

There's another story along this line about a little girl who prayed, "O God, I ask You to be sure not to let the beautiful birds get into Jimmy Brown's trap. Jimmy is a nice boy, but he has a very cruel trap. Dear God, I am going to count on You not to let any birds get into his trap. Amen."

The little girl's mother heard the prayer and inquired, "Why are you so sure that God will keep the birds safe?" The child replied, "I know God will because He helped me bust the trap!"

People often come up to me and say, "Lowell, will you please pray that I'll get a job?" I'll say, "Certainly. But have you been looking for a job?" They often reply, "No." I have noticed that God does not answer their prayers because they are lazy.

When Abraham's chief servant was sent to find a bride for Isaac, he said, "...*I BEING IN THE WAY, the Lord led me...*"[24] In other words, when he headed down the highway, God began to lead him.

The Bible says that as the early disciples "...*went forth, and preached every where, the Lord* [worked] *with them...confirming the word with signs following...*"[25] The signs will follow you, too. SO STEP OUT! Pray the promises of God. Pray in Jesus' name, and pray specifically. When you follow these scriptural principles, your prayers will penetrate heaven.

Scripture References

1	Hebrews 4:16	14	Psalm 2:8
2	Romans 8:37	15	Matthew 6:8
3	John 16:23,24	16	John 11:43
4	Philippians 2:9-11	17	Mark 10:46,47
5	Acts 19:13-16	18	Mark 10:49
6	John 14:14	19	Mark 10:51
7	Luke 10:19	20	Mark 10:52
8	Mark 16:17,18	21	Matthew 18:18
9	Isaiah 41:21	22	Matthew 6:10
10	Isaiah 43:26	23	Revelation 1:6
11	Philippians 4:13	24	Genesis 24:27
12	Colossians 2:10	25	Mark 16:20
13	Matthew 28:20		

CHAPTER ELEVEN

Praying the Prayer of Faith

How much time do you spend in prayer each day? Please check one:

☐ One hour.
☐ Thirty minutes.
☐ Fifteen minutes.
☐ Five minutes.

What is your answer? It will determine what is going to happen to your life. Every notable Christian I've ever met or read about was a man or woman of prayer.

I have been shocked and saddened by the results of a survey I have been conducting throughout the United States and Canada for the past five years. Approximately a quarter of a million Christians from various denominations attend our services each year and, as I've mentioned earlier, *only one in ten reads the Bible and prays even as little as ten minutes per day.*

Surveys by other organizations show that the average Christian family in the U.S. has the TV set turned on more than five hours a day. Is it any wonder that the devil's power is growing stronger and many Christians are growing weaker?

"It is quite natural and inevitable," writes Dean Inge, "that if we spend 16 hours daily of our waking life in thinking about the affairs of the world, and five minutes in thinking about God...this world will seem 200 times more real to us than God."

There is a definite correspondence between the amount of time you spend in prayer and the degree of victory you have over temptation. The Lord's disciples did not realize the importance of prayer, and when the real test came, they all forsook Jesus. Peter even cursed to show that he was not one of the Lord's followers.[1]

Your prayer time is the most important hour of the day—it cannot be put off!

One wise Christian observed, "We say we are too busy to pray. But the busier our Lord was, the more He prayed." Martin Luther, when asked what his plans were for the following day, answered, "Work, work, and more work from early until late. In fact, I have so much to do that I shall spend the first three hours in prayer."

Christian men who have shaken our world have been men of passionate prayer! Dr. Adoniram Judson, a spiritual giant, said, "Arrange thy affairs, if possible, so that thou canst leisurely devote two or three hours every day not merely to devotional exercises but to the very act of secret prayer and communion with God." John Bunyan, author of the world-changing book, *The Pilgrim's Progress*, penned, "He who runs from God in the morning will scarcely find Him the rest of the day." St. Patrick recorded in his *Confessions*, "In a single day I have prayed as many as a hundred times, and in the night almost as often."

I have been an evangelist of the Gospel for almost twenty-four years, and God has taught me many things. But the greatest lessons have been in prayer. At first I thought my chief purpose was to preach for decisions. I declared the power of Jesus Christ to save, and thousands of people responded to my messages every year.

But then God showed me other needs in people's lives and directed me to preach self-help sermons. So I began to show people how to overcome fear, lust, envy, greed and other works of the flesh.

Within the past year, however, the Lord has shown me that people have a need nearly as great as salvation and more basic than victory over the flesh. THEY NEED TO LEARN HOW TO PRAY! I believe George Herbert is right when he says, "Resort to sermons, but to prayers most: Praying's the end of preaching."

I want to preach each sermon so that when I finish people will cry out to God in prayer. If they are lost, they will not make just temporary, cold-hearted decisions to follow Jesus Christ, they will call out to God in sincere repentance. Often when John Wesley preached, the cries of penitent sinners drowned the sound of his voice. I want to see the Holy Spirit convict lost men and women of their need for God. This is why I commit my messages to God in prayer. Down through the years I have often seen men and women run forward to receive Jesus Christ even before I have given the invitation! If people are already saved and committed to Jesus Christ, I want them to respond to my message by calling upon God for a fresh touch of His Spirit on their lives.

If you are a minister, remember that most of your congregation is made up of non-praying people. Always remember that only one in ten spends as little as ten minutes a day in earnest prayer. The only way you will be able to lead your congregation to God in prayer is by truly becoming a man of prayer yourself.

In 2 Corinthians 3:5,6, the Apostle Paul points out the danger of preaching sermons that are not fired by prayer: *"...our sufficiency is of God; who also hath made us able ministers of the new testament; not of the LETTER, but of the*

SPIRIT: FOR THE LETTER KILLETH, BUT THE SPIRIT GIVETH LIFE." I am convinced that many sincere Christian leaders do not see life-changing results in their ministries because they are preaching dead-letter sermons to non-praying people.

When an editor of the London *Times* asked Charles Spurgeon for permission to publish his sermons, the famous preacher said, "Go ahead. You can print my sermons, BUT YOU CAN'T PRINT MY FIRE." The writer to the Hebrews says, *"...Our God is a consuming fire."*[2] People need to feel His holy fire, but they won't until it becomes a roaring flame within your own soul. Sincere and earnest prayer is the only way to keep your heart white hot for God!

Beware of thinking of yourself as a Bible teacher, a pastor or spiritual counselor

While it may be true that you are called to be an evangelist, Bible teacher or counselor, above all else you are called to be a man of prayer. Paul adds one more responsibility.

He wrote to the young pastor, Timothy, *"...DO THE WORK OF AN EVANGELIST, make full proof of thy ministry."*[3]

Within the past two decades, I have been honored to make friends of more than a thousand pastors. During private conversations with these men of God, I have urged them to arouse their congregations to earnestly seek God in prayer. But many pastors have smiled and replied, "Lowell, I'm not an evangelist; I am a pastor." I know that in saying this some have dismissed their responsibility to enthusiastically lead their people in prayer.

Paul stressed to Timothy, *"...I put thee in remembrance that thou STIR UP THE GIFT OF GOD, WHICH IS IN THEE...."*[4] The Apostle Peter said, *"...I think it meet* [appropriate], *as long as I am in this tabernacle* [body], *to STIR YOU UP by putting you in remembrance...."*[5]

As a minister, you are responsible to stir people up to pray. You are the undershepherd, and your sheep follow in your footsteps. They won't pray more than you do! Beware of spending more time in sermon preparation than in prayer. Words without the Spirit will kill.

I can tell you from personal experience that prayer is often hard work. But prayer determines whether spiritual battles are won or lost. As soldiers of Jesus Christ, we should be hard on ourselves. General William Booth of the Salvation Army once said that if he could he would have finalized the training of his soldiers by hanging them over hell for 24 hours.

Leonard Ravenhill says, "Let any man shut himself up for a week with only bread and water, with no books except the Bible, with no visitor except the Holy Ghost, and I guarantee (you) my preaching brethren that that man will either break up or break through and out. After that, like Paul, he will be known in hell!"

Satan is playing hardball, and many Christians don't even know it. When the game gets rough, they drop out and go home. But you and I have sufficient power to defeat Satan with our prayers. Our weapons are *"...mighty through God to the pulling down of strong holds...."*[6] The Apostle John encourages us: *"...greater is he that is in you, than he that is in the world."*[7] Whether you are a minister or a layman, you can take steps to increase the effectiveness of your prayers.

Be persuaded that prayer really works

You must have faith in God's promises; *"...without faith it is impossible to please him: for he that cometh to God MUST believe that he is, AND THAT HE IS A REWARDER OF THEM THAT DILIGENTLY SEEK HIM."*[8]

Gerald Vann says, "Some people think that prayer just means asking for things, and if they fail to receive exactly what they asked for, they think the whole thing is a fraud." Do you *really* believe that God is going to answer your prayers? If you do, you have unlocked unlimited opportunities. Jesus says, *"...with God ALL THINGS ARE POSSIBLE."*[9] *"...ALL THINGS ARE POSSIBLE TO HIM THAT BELIEVETH."*[10] If you believe these two Bible verses, then through faith everything that is possible for God is possible for you.

If you hesitate at heaven's door, you will go away empty-handed. The Apostle James says, *"If any of you lack...let him ask of God, that giveth to all men liberally.... BUT let him ask in faith, NOTHING WAVERING. For he that wavereth is like a wave of the sea driven with the wind and tossed. ...LET NOT THAT MAN THINK THAT HE SHALL RECEIVE ANY THING FROM THE LORD."*[11]

If you want to pray with power and get results, you must pray in faith. James states, *"...THE PRAYER OF FAITH shall save the sick, and the Lord shall raise him up."*[12] The problem with many prayers today is that they are prayed in unbelief.

Recently I visited a dear Christian brother who was suffering from poor health and had not been outside of his home for months. He was terribly depressed and bitter because he had not been healed. He said, "I pray, but it doesn't do any good." I tried to point out that he had been praying in unbelief. The prayer of FAITH shall save the sick— prayers of unbelief go unanswered.

Do you believe that God will reward those who diligently seek Him? If you don't believe that prayer can be effective, try an experiment. Invest 15 minutes a day in prayer about your problems. Keep this up for 30 days and see if your prayers haven't made a difference. I know they will. Archbishop Temple told critics of prayer, "When I pray, coincidences happen. When I do not, they don't."

But the matter of praying in faith leads us to a deeper question.

How can you develop your faith so that you will pray believing prayers?

The answer is this: by becoming a student of God's Word. Every man and woman who has been successful in prayer has also been a devoted student of the Scriptures. IT IS TRUE, *"...FAITH COMETH BY HEARING, AND HEARING BY THE WORD OF GOD."*[13] Your prayers will have power in direct ratio to the amount of time you spend in earnest study of God's Word. *God's Word is the fuel for your faith*. The more that God's promises become part of your life, the greater your faith will become.

Smith Wigglesworth reflects, "There is one thing that God has given me from my youth up—a taste and relish for the Bible. I can say before God, I have never read a book but my Bible, so I know nothing about books. It seems to me better to get the Book of books for food for your soul, for the strengthening of your faith, and the building up of your character in God, so that all the time you are being changed and made meet to walk with God.

"And remember, God wants daring men, men who will dare all, men who will be strong in Him and dare to do exploits. How shall we reach this plane of faith? *Let go of your own thoughts, and take the thoughts of God*, the Word of God. If you build up yourself on imaginations you will go wrong. You have the Word of God and it is enough. A man gave this remarkable testimony concerning the Word: *(Please read the following statement out loud. I have done so many times. God anoints it to my spirit in a special way.—Lowell)*

" 'NEVER COMPARE THIS BOOK WITH OTHER BOOKS. COMPARISONS ARE DANGEROUS. NEVER THINK OR NEVER SAY THAT THIS BOOK CONTAINS THE WORD OF GOD. *IT IS THE WORD OF*

GOD. IT IS SUPERNATURAL IN ORIGIN, ETERNAL IN DURATION, INEXPRESS-IBLE IN VALUE, INFINITE IN SCOPE, RE-GENERATIVE IN POWER, INFALLIBLE IN AUTHORITY, UNIVERSAL IN INTER-EST, PERSONAL IN APPLICATION, IN-SPIRED IN TOTALITY. READ IT THROUGH. WRITE IT DOWN. PRAY IT IN. WORK IT OUT. AND THEN PASS IT ON.'"

Hallelujah! God's Word has the power to turn your life and mine into living epistles of His grace. God's Word has power to ener-gize the 100 billion brain cells of your mind until you are alive with eternal truth. God's Word has the power to enable you—from the deepest region of your soul—to BE-LIEVE HIS PROMISES!

The Lord instructs us, *"It is the spirit that quickeneth; the flesh profiteth nothing: THE WORDS THAT I SPEAK UNTO YOU, THEY ARE SPIRIT, AND THEY ARE LIFE."* [14] *"...IF YE CONTINUE IN MY WORD, then are ye my disciples indeed; AND YE SHALL KNOW THE TRUTH, AND THE TRUTH SHALL MAKE YOU FREE."* [15] As you hunger for God's Word, study it and feast upon it prayerfully, the Scriptures will impart the life of God to you. As you fill your mind with the eternal truths of God, you will be liberated from your doubts.

I like to study the Bible and good books that explain and apply the Scriptures to everyday life. As I continue to feed my mind and soul with God's promises, my soul soon bursts forth with praises to God. When our family is at home, my wife, Connie, and our children will sometimes hear me shouting, "Hallelujah!" three rooms away. I can pray easily when I'm buoyed up by God's promises. When God's Word is aflame in my heart the Holy Spirit enables me to pray prayers of faith.

I used to think that the amount of time I spent in prayer might be a little excessive until I began to study the biographies of evangelists who were greatly used of God. Rowland Hill, for example, was a British evangelist who won thousands of people to Jesus Christ. One day Charles Spurgeon visited Rowland Hill's estate. Spurgeon asked his guide where the famous evangelist spent his time in Bible study and prayer. The guide, who had been a friend of Dr. Hill, replied, "The fact is, we never found any. Mr. Hill used to study in the garden, in the parlor, in the bedroom, in the streets, in the woods, anywhere."

Then Spurgeon asked, "Where did he pray?" The man answered, "We're not sure exactly. He was always praying. Sometimes he would stand in Blackfriars Road with his hand under his coattails, looking in a shop window. But under his breath he'd be praying. You could hear him if you got close enough. Mr. Hill was always praying."

ALWAYS REMEMBER THAT FAITH COMES BY HEARING GOD'S WORD. Reading the Scriptures is not enough—you need to confess them with your lips. As you hear the Word of God from your own lips, your faith will be strengthened.

Your words are important. If you spend the day talking about worldly things and seldom mention the Lord except in passing, you will hardly be able to pray the prayer of faith. But if you memorize and repeat God's Word out loud, you will soon have the mind of Jesus Christ. As Paul instructs, *"Let this mind be in you, which was also in Christ Jesus...."*[16]

You will receive the mind of Christ as you study the Holy Scriptures under the guidance of the Holy Spirit. When Satan confronted Jesus Christ in the wilderness, Jesus defeated the devil with the written Word of God. At the same time, Jesus guaranteed our victory over sin. As you confront temptation and satanic resistance, *"...take...the sword of the Spirit, which is the word of God: praying always...in the Spirit...."*[17] You will win your battles!

If you believe that God rewards those who seek Him, if you desire to please God by praying in faith, DO NOT ALLOW ANYTHING TO COME BETWEEN YOU AND THE WORD OF GOD. Study the Bible, search it, confess it, memorize it, rehearse it and cherish it until your faith rises like a rocket for the stars. *"...ALL THINGS ARE POSSIBLE TO HIM THAT BELIEVETH."*[18]

Scripture References

1   See Matthew 26:74
2   Hebrews 12:29
3   2 Timothy 4:5
4   2 Timothy 1:6
5   2 Peter 1:13
6   2 Corinthians 10:4
7   1 John 4:4
8   Hebrews 11:6
9   Matthew 19:26
10   Mark 9:23
11   James 1:5-7
12   James 5:15
13   Romans 10:17
14   John 6:63
15   John 8:31,32
16   Philippians 2:5
17   Ephesians 6:17,18
18   Mark 9:23

CHAPTER TWELVE

Binding Satan Through Prayer

Satan is your archenemy, and don't ever forget it. The Apostle Peter warns, *"Be sober, be vigilant; because your adversary the devil, as a roaring lion, walketh about, seeking whom he may devour: whom resist steadfast in the faith...."*[1]

The Living Bible paraphrases the same two verses, *"Be careful—watch out for attacks from Satan, YOUR GREAT ENEMY. He prowls around like a hungry, roaring lion, looking for some victim to tear apart. Stand firm when he attacks. Trust the Lord; and remember that other Christians all around the world are going through these sufferings too."*

Step One in defeating Satan is to have a good hold of the Scriptures

Although Satan is strong, God has not left you defenseless. Paul says, *"Put on the whole armor of God, that ye may be able to stand against the wiles of the devil."*[2] God has not only given you armor for protection, He has given you one great offensive weapon. Paul instructs you to *"...take...the sword of the Spirit, which is the word of God."*[3]

The Bible is your offensive weapon in your war against Satan. Once you know how to use it, God's Word is more than sufficient to defeat the devil. The Apostle James assures you, *"...Resist the devil, and he will flee from you."*[4]

Satan fears the Word of God more than anything else because the truth will overwhelm him. This is why he is doing everything he can to snatch the Word of God from your heart. Jesus says, *"When any one heareth the word of the kingdom, and understandeth it not, then cometh the wicked one, and catcheth away that which was sown in his heart...."*[5]

When you are filled with God's truth, you are armed for spiritual warfare. To neutralize your power in Christ, the devil is doing everything possible to destroy your times of Bible study. He attempts to distract you with television programs, secular music, visiting friends, work and recreation. In order to turn your mind from the Word of God, Satan will even entice you with *good* things to do, *"...for Satan himself is transformed into an angel of light."*[6] If the devil succeeds in destroying your time for prayer and Bible study, he will have destroyed your effectiveness for Christ.

Step Two in overcoming the evil one is to know how to bind him with prayer

F. J. Huegel says, "Much of the Savior's ministry and teaching will remain for us an unsolved riddle if we fail to grasp the significance of this great fact of prayer warfare against the powers of darkness. No man can enter into a strong man's house and spoil his goods, except he will first bind the strong man: and then he will spoil his house, our Lord tells us. Only when Satan is bound and defeated are we assured of answered prayer."

Satan is the third party involved in your prayers. When you pray, Satan will try to impede your efforts to concentrate on God. For this reason, you should pray in and with the Holy Spirit. God gave the prophet, Zechariah, a vision of the spiritual struggle in prayer. The prophet relates, "...he [God] showed me Joshua the high priest standing before the angel of the Lord, and SATAN STANDING AT HIS RIGHT HAND TO RESIST HIM."[7]

If you feel an unseen struggle at prayer time, you know what's happening—Satan is resisting you. This is why Paul says we need to be "...praying always with all prayer and supplication IN THE SPIRIT...AND... WITH ALL PERSEVERANCE...."[8] As you wrestle in prayer with the depressing, opposing forces of hell, the Holy Spirit will help you to overcome and your prayers will penetrate heaven.

At one point in Christ's ministry, the Pharisees accused Him of casting out evil spirits by the devil's power. Jesus replied, *"...if Satan cast out Satan, he is divided against himself; how shall then his kingdom stand?"* Then He added, *"But if I cast out devils by the Spirit of God* [Notice His reference to defeating devils by the Spirit of God], *then the kingdom of God is come unto you. Or else, how can one enter into a strong man's house, and spoil his goods, except he first bind the strong man? and then he will spoil his house."*[9] If you want to pray effectively, tearing down the devil's strongholds, you must first bind the strong man in prayer.

Some Christians operate in exactly the opposite way. They hope that if they don't mention the devil he will go away. But the devil won't give up an inch of ground unless he has to. Your prayers in the Spirit, based upon the promises of God's Word, will guarantee that he has to give way!

For years I have bound the devil and pled the blood of Jesus Christ in prayer. Here's why. Paul teaches, *"...now in Christ Jesus ye who sometimes were far off are made nigh* [close to God] *BY THE BLOOD OF CHRIST. For he is our peace,...who hath broken down the middle wall of partition between us...."*[10]

The writer to the Jewish Christians pointed out how important the blood of Jesus is to prayer: "[We have]...*boldness to enter into the holiest BY THE BLOOD OF JESUS.*"[11] When you plead the power of the blood over a situation, you have immediate access to the throne of God.

Plead the blood!

About seven years ago, God showed my brother, Larry, and his wife, Gloria, the dramatic power of Jesus' blood. They were driving their old bus through the flatlands of South Dakota on a dark, starless night. Gloria had been "riding shotgun" to help keep Larry awake but finally said, "Honey, I've just got to go to bed and get some sleep."

She relates, "I fell asleep so fast and hard I felt like I'd died. For me that was unusual because through the years I've had a terrible time trying to sleep on the bus. Whenever the driver took a sharp corner or applied the brakes, I'd wake up.

"It was 4:00 a.m., and I was sleeping soundly, totally unaware of anything around me. All of a sudden I lurched forward to a sitting position, and the Holy Spirit seemed to shout, 'Plead the blood!' In a split second, I was wide awake, hearing my own voice command, 'I plead the blood in the name of Jesus! I plead the blood in the name of Jesus!'

"As soon as I completed the last word, I felt the brakes of the bus grab. Every piece of metal and wood fought the force of gravity, and then the bus swerved sharply. I kept saying, 'Jesus, Jesus.' To my surprise, the bus came back under control. I knew one thing for certain—God had awakened me to plead the blood over our bus and lives.

"I jumped out of bed, ran up the aisle and said, 'Larry, I was back there sound asleep and the Holy Spirit woke me up to plead the blood. What happened?'

"Larry replied, 'My headlights picked up the figures of five or six horses going across the road. They were in formation like a group of Ringling Brothers Circus elephants, tails and trunks across the entire highway! There was no way I could stop the bus fast enough to miss them, so I looked for the smallest horse to hit. Do you know what?

That horse hesitated and opened a path just wide enough for the bus to run through!'

"Then I knew why God woke me up. When I prayed, 'I plead the blood in the name of Jesus!' the horse hesitated and opened a way for the bus to go through, saving us from what could have been a fatal accident. Praise God—there is power in the blood of Jesus!"

During the early part of my ministry, an elderly Methodist pastor from Watertown, South Dakota, gave me some good advice. He said to never forget the blood of Jesus when I lead inquirers in the sinner's prayer. His words, "Lowell, don't forget the blood!" were imprinted on my mind. Since then, this godly minister has gone on to heaven. I often think of him when I stand before a crowd of people who have pressed forward to be converted. I like to imagine that when the angels rejoice over these souls, the Lord assures His dear servant, "Lowell still remembers the blood. He hasn't forgotten your advice."

Armed with God's Word, praying in the Spirit and pleading the blood of Jesus Christ, you have all the authority and power you need to bind the devil. Jesus said to Peter, *"...thou art Peter* [petros, a stone], *and upon this rock* [petra, a huge, solid rock, referring to Jesus Christ Himself] *I will build my church; and THE GATES OF HELL SHALL NOT PREVAIL AGAINST IT."*[12]

I will never forget the time we conducted a youth camp in Wisconsin. Hundreds of teen-agers attended, but God began to deal with one young lady in particular. She told me later that she had been rebellious toward her parents, the people of her church and her teachers at school for a long time. The Bible says, *"...rebellion is as the sin of witchcraft...."*[13] When a person rebels against authority, he opens himself to Satan.

Many young people were turning to Jesus Christ in the camp meetings. The night before, we'd prayed for a young lady who hadn't been able to sleep for months. Evil spirits would come into her room, rattle the windows and throw objects off of the dresser. God delivered her, and this evening she testified that she was now able to sleep without fear of demonic annoyances.

The girl whom God had been dealing with couldn't take it any longer. She jumped up and ran out of the building. Then she screamed, "Satan, take over my life!" He did. Evil spirits began to spew blasphemies from her mouth and she writhed as though she'd lost her mind. The evil spirits were in control.

Several camp counselors helped her to a cabin and began to pray. About two hundred teens surrounded the cabin, prayed strong prayers in the Spirit and pled the blood of Jesus.

I was still conducting the service when one of the camp workers came and told me what was happening. In that moment, the Spirit of God came mightily upon me. I could feel a surge of power and authority beyond my own.

Relating the story of the actual exorcism of the evil spirits would take more space that I can devote to this chapter. But as the last demon left, he shrieked through her lips, "I can't win! I'm getting out of here!" Freed, the young lady began to worship and praise God. The Lord had delivered her!

Two years later we returned to the camp for meetings and saw her once more. She had grown strong in the Lord and become a counselor, helping other teen-aged girls. Today she is a victorious Christian, thanks to the power of prayer!

The evil spirit's parting words are worth remembering: "I can't win! I'm getting out of here!" The Apostle James says, "...the devils...believe, and tremble."14 As a child of God, you can take authority over Satan with the Word of God. As you pray in the Spirit and plead the blood of Jesus Christ, you don't have to cower—YOU CAN COMMAND!

Jesus says, "...Whatsoever ye shall bind on earth shall be bound in heaven: and whatsoever ye shall loose on earth shall be loosed in heaven."15 You hold the keys to binding the strong man. If you allow Satan to run loose in your affairs, he will. But if you issue a command-prayer, God and all of heaven will stand behind you and Satan will be bound.

A close friend of mine recently told me that an evil spirit had made his little girl totally rebellious. He said that as he prayed and bound Satan, she was delivered and her personality changed 180 degrees to the good.

Years ago we conducted a church crusade in Two Harbors, Minnesota. I recognized a spiritual bondage in the meetings, and I knew we were under satanic attack. One night before the meeting, I prayed earnestly in the pastor's study, and the Lord opened my spiritual eyes. I could see black spirits surrounding the church. Suddenly the white spirits—angels—appeared and drove the demons away. Instantly God's Spirit poured into my soul. That night there was a great spiritual victory, and the crusade continued for three weeks. Christians experienced revival and many unbelievers were won to Jesus Christ.

For the past two decades, we have conducted more than one hundred one-night rallies a year. WE HAVE FOUND—BY ACTUAL COUNT—THAT WHEN THERE IS CONCENTRATED PRAYER FOR THE ONE-NIGHT CRUSADE RALLIES, THREE TIMES AS MANY PEOPLE ARE WON TO JESUS CHRIST. Approximately fifty people make decisions for the Lord during an average rally. But about one hundred fifty people go forward to dedicate their lives to Jesus Christ during a rally that has been spiritually prepared—where Satan has been bound and sinners set free from his grasp.

Your prayers enable God to win the lost in special ways

Jesus told His disciples, *"...The harvest truly is plenteous, but the laborers are few; PRAY YE therefore the Lord of the harvest, that he will send forth laborers into his harvest."*[16] Now, here is a puzzling question. If the Lord is not willing that any should perish but that all be saved,[17] why do you need to pray that the Lord will send laborers into the harvest?

Although God is willing—and desirous—to save the lost, He will not overrule His church. We are His agency on earth. If we refuse to pray, God will not move. This fact places an awesome responsibility upon your shoulders and mine. We *must* pray for the evangelization of the world—for missions, for every God-directed evangelistic thrust.

Intercession before the throne of grace could be your greatest ministry! The Bible says that Anna, 84 years of age, *"...departed not from the temple, but served God with fastings and prayers night and day."*[18]

Sandra Goodwin has written these meaningful lines:

TRAVELING ON MY KNEES

Last night I took a journey
To a land across the seas.
I didn't go by ship or plane—
I traveled on my knees.

I saw so many people there
In bondage to their sin,
And Jesus told me I should go,
That there were souls to win.

But I said, "Jesus, I can't go
To lands across the seas."
He answered quickly, "Yes, you can—
By traveling on your knees."

He said, "You pray, I'll meet the need.
You call, and I will hear.
It's up to you to be concerned
For lost souls far and near."

And so I did; I knelt in prayer,
Gave up some hours of ease,
And with the Savior by my side
I traveled on my knees.

As I prayed on, I saw souls saved
And twisted persons healed.
I saw God's workers' strength renewed
While laboring on the field.

I said, "Yes, Lord, I'll take the job.
Your heart I want to please.
I'll heed Your call and swiftly go
By traveling on my knees."

I believe we are going to see a great increase of satanic activity in these last days. The devil knows that his time is short. The battle that is raging between the forces of righteousness and evil will culminate during the Tribulation which will soon sweep over the world.

Jesus warns, *"...then shall be great tribulation, such as was not since the beginning of the world to this time, no, nor ever shall be. And except those days should be shortened, there should no flesh be saved: but for the elect's sake those days shall be shortened."*[19] I personally believe that Jesus Christ will return for His true church before this terrible time. (I explain this prophetic period in greater detail in my book, *The Wind Whispers Warning.*)

The Apostle John had a vision of what will happen in the heavens during the latter part of the Great Tribulation. Read carefully:

"...there was war in heaven: Michael and his angels fought against the dragon [Satan]*; and the*

dragon fought and his angels, and prevailed not; neither was their place found any more in heaven.

"And the great dragon was cast out, that old serpent, called the Devil, and Satan, which deceiveth the whole world: he was cast out into the earth, and his angels were cast out with him.

"And I heard a loud voice saying in heaven, Now is come salvation, and strength, and the kingdom of our God, and the power of his Christ: FOR THE ACCUSER OF OUR BRETHREN is cast down, which accused them before our God day and night."[20]

Do you realize that Satan is constantly accusing you before the throne of God? This is why Jesus Christ became our High Priest. He constantly intercedes for us. According to the Bible, *"...this man [Jesus Christ], because he continueth ever, hath an unchangeable priesthood. Wherefore he is able also to save them to the uttermost that come unto God by him, seeing he ever liveth to make intercession for them."*[21]

Prayer is both powerful and necessary!

For nearly two thousand years, the full-time ministry of Jesus Christ has been intercession for the saints. When Satan steps up to the throne to accuse you, Jesus immediately intercedes on your behalf. *Let's do OUR part by praying for others!*

The Apostle John relates, *"...they* [the church] *overcame him* [the devil] *by the blood of the Lamb, and by the word of their testimony; and they loved not their lives unto the death.*

"Therefore rejoice, ye heavens, and ye that dwell in them. Woe to the inhabiters of the earth and of the sea! FOR THE DEVIL IS COME DOWN UNTO YOU, HAVING GREAT WRATH, BECAUSE HE KNOWETH THAT HE HATH BUT A SHORT TIME."[22]

Thanks be to God—He has given us the victory! You will win your battles by the power of the blood, by the Word of God which should be your testimony, and by the might of the Holy Spirit.

Use your power to ATTACK! Claim the lost souls that belong to the Lord. You will never win a popularity contest with the devil by backing away in fear. He only acknowledges power. God has supplied you with all the power you need.

If you don't feel that you have appropriated enough power yet, spend more time in the Scriptures and prayer. Pray until your soul is on fire and study until you know how to wield your sword, God's Word. The battle lines are drawn. With Jesus Christ interceding for us in heaven, we are more than conquerors!

Scripture References

1 *1 Peter 5:8,9*
2 *Ephesians 6:11*
3 *Ephesians 6:17*
4 *James 4:7*
5 *Matthew 13:19*
6 *2 Corinthians 11:14*
7 *Zechariah 3:1*
8 *Ephesians 6:18*
9 *Matthew 12:26-29*
10 *Ephesians 2:13,14*
11 *Hebrews 10:19*
12 *Matthew 16:18*
13 *1 Samuel 15:23*
14 *James 2:19*
15 *Matthew 18:18*
16 *Matthew 9:37,38*
17 *See 2 Peter 3:9*
18 *Luke 2:37*
19 *Matthew 24:21,22*
20 *Revelation 12:7-10*
21 *Hebrews 7:24-25*
22 *Revelation 12:11,12*

CHAPTER THIRTEEN

Hangups That Hinder Prayer

Many people have hangups that keep them from praying until a crisis. The story is told of a sailor who was on board a sinking ship. In an almost hopeless effort to save themselves, he and the rest of the crew launched a lifeboat. Hurricane winds tossed the little boat in 15-foot waves. Realizing that the end was near, the sailor crawled to the bow of the lifeboat and prayed, "O God, I've never bothered You in 40 years, and if You get me out of this mess I'll never bother You again!"

A Christian man once said, "God sometimes *leads* men into the prayer life. Sometimes, however, God has to *drive* us into such a life." George Buttrick remarked,

"Critics sometimes deride prayer by speaking of it as 'foxhole religion.' But what *if* our planet *is* a foxhole?"

In one way or another, God is determined that you and I become people of prayer. Have you ever stopped to consider that many of the problems and crises we face are allowed to help us overcome our hangups about prayer? Samuel Rutherford wrote, "Oh, what I owe to the furnace, the file and hammer of my Lord Jesus."

There is a tremendous difference between two of Jesus' disciples—Judas and Simon Peter. Both men denied the Lord and felt sorry, but Judas went out and hanged himself whereas Peter repented and prayed. I believe that Peter turned back to the Lord because he had spent much time with Jesus in prayer, so he knew the Lord better than Judas did. The Scriptures record, "...*Satan entered into him* [Judas]..."[1] and "...*it had been good for that man if he had not been born.*"[2]

A prayerless life will catch up with a man. Bishop Arthur J. Moore tells of a man who jumped to his death from the window of a skyscraper. An old black janitor who knew the man commented sadly, "When a man has lost God, there ain't nothing to do but jump."

You must overcome whatever hinders your prayers! Unbelief will keep you from seeking God. There is tremendous power in prayer. When the A-bomb was dropped on Hiroshima on August 6, 1945, more than ninety-two thousand Japanese died. In contrast, when King Sennacherib's mighty Assyrian army invaded the tiny nation of Judah in 701 B.C. and surrounded Jerusalem, Judah's king, Hezekiah, looked to God for help. He took the Assyrian monarch's threat letter into the temple, "...*spread it before the Lord.*"[3] and prayed.

In answer to Hezekiah's prayer, the angel of the Lord destroyed 185,000 Assyrian soldiers in one night. The rest fled for their lives. When Sennacherib returned to Nineveh, his own sons murdered him.[4] Hezekiah's prayer triggered power that destroyed 185,000 Assyrians—MORE THAN TWICE THE POWER OF THE FIRST ATOMIC ATTACK! Don't ever forget that your prayers are more powerful than A-bombs. No wonder the devil is trying to keep you from seeking God for help!

Let's discuss some of the hangups that hinder prayer.

The problem of praying out loud in a group

According to a recent survey, the number-one fear of Americans today is neither the fear of death (That ranks sixth) nor the fear of losing one's health (That ranks second). The number-one fear is giving a speech before a group of people.

Many people have a hangup about praying out loud among a group of Christians. They fear criticism, and this feeling is compounded by the seriousness of addressing God.

How can you overcome the fear of standing in public and praying out loud? Realize that your pride may be your hangup. W. E. Zimmerman says, "Many young Christians say, 'I can pray when alone, but I cannot pray in public.' The big reason for this is they are praying to please people instead of God."

Beware of the superstar syndrome!

Many people compare their first efforts in group prayer with the prayers of Christians who are more accustomed to praying aloud. New Christians often value others' gifts of gab and memorized phraseology too highly.

Remember, you don't have to speed pray like some spiritual machine gunner, and you don't have to pray fancy phrases. Samuel Chadwick reminds us, "The great souls that pray hours a day were once beginners." They simply grew as they matured in Jesus Christ. Chadwick also says, "*A cry brings God. A cry is mightier than the polished phrase.*"

If you are afraid of praying in public, incorporate your fears into your prayers. Be honest. You could pray, "Father in heaven, thanks for saving my soul. You know I don't know much about praying in public, and I'm scared to death, but I love You and I love these people, and I want You to answer these requests. Thank You, God, for what You are going to do. In Jesus' name, amen."

Frankly, some of the most beautiful prayers I have ever heard have been prayed by our 2- and 3-year-old children—and by new Christians. A pastor told me about a young man who thrilled the members of his church by praying for his dance band. The newly converted entertainer prayed, "O God, please help my band members to 'get the bug' (a slang expression meaning *to desire change*)." God understands and appreciates beginners' prayers, and Christians love them too.

Quiet and loud prayers

I have noticed that some people do not think praying aloud is necessary, but the Scriptures teach us that a deep desire is accompanied by loud prayers. There are times, however, when quiet prayers are in order. During the presidency of Lyndon Johnson, Bill Moyers, the President's press secretary (a Baptist minister), was asked to offer the mealtime prayer. He began by praying quietly. President Johnson became some-

what irritated and interrupted him. He said,
"Pray louder!" The press secretary looked
up and replied, "I'm sorry, sir, but I wasn't
addressing you."

There are times when loud prayers are out
of order. However, many people who pray
quietly do not think that they could muster
the courage to pray loudly enough to be
heard in a group even if they wanted to.

King David said, *"This poor man CRIED,
and the Lord heard him...."*[5] According to
Strong's Concordance, another synonym for
the Hebrew word for *cried* is *screamed*. Therefore, David says that when he *screamed*, the
Lord heard him.

People say, "The Lord isn't deaf, so why
should we scream to Him?" The answer is
that the Lord isn't nervous either! The Apostle James declares, *"...The effectual FERVENT
PRAYER of a righteous man availeth much."*[6]

Consider blind Bartimaeus. He wanted
healing so badly that when Jesus walked by
*"...he began to cry out, and say, Jesus, thou son of
David, have mercy on me."*[7] But when you begin to call out to the Lord in fervent prayer,
there's usually someone around who wants
you to quiet down. Bartimaeus endured the

same criticism. The Apostle Mark records, *"...many charged him that he should hold his peace: BUT HE CRIED THE MORE A GREAT DEAL.... AND JESUS STOOD STILL...."*[8] Bartimaeus reached Jesus by praying loudly.

King David declares, *"My tongue shall sing ALOUD of your righteousness.... O Lord, open my lips, and my mouth shall show forth your praise."*[9] According to the Scriptures, the early Christians also prayed out loud and with great power. After Peter and John were released from custody for healing the man at the Beautiful Gate, they returned to their prayer group and reported the threats of the chief priests and elders.[10] *"And when they heard that, THEY LIFTED UP THEIR VOICE TO GOD WITH ONE ACCORD...."*[11]

Jesus, *"...in the days of his flesh...OFFERED UP PRAYERS AND SUPPLICATIONS WITH STRONG CRYING AND TEARS...."*[12] The Greek noun, *krauge*, literally means *crying* in this verse. The verb, *krazo*, is quite similar, meaning *to cry out*, and applies to inarticulate cries from fear or pain.

King David prayed, *"Lord, I cry unto thee: make haste unto me; give ear unto my voice, when I cry unto thee. Let my prayer be set forth before*

*thee as incense; and the lifting up of my hands as
the evening sacrifice.''*[13]

When Jesus and His disciples made their
way into Jerusalem on the day that is now
remembered as Palm Sunday, *''...the disciples began to rejoice and praise God with a loud
voice...saying, Blessed be the King that cometh in
the name of the Lord....''*[14] But the cold-
hearted Pharisees who were following them
told Jesus, *''...Master, rebuke thy disciples.''*[15]
Jesus responded, *''...I tell you that, if these
should hold their peace, the stones would immediately cry out.''*[16]

God had poured His Spirit upon the multitude and they praised the Lord. It was right
for Jesus to be worshiped loudly—He was
coming as King! When we worship God
with a congregation that is caught up in an
orchestration of praise, you and I should
raise our voices and praise God loudly, with
all our hearts, because our worship is directed by none other than the Holy Spirit
Himself.

A lukewarm minister once announced
that he was going to preach a sermon attacking the many people who claim that God
works miracles today. In order to obtain the

necessary source material he needed for his message, he attended a meeting conducted by a fiery evangelist.

As he listened to the great man of God preach, the minister came under conviction and realized that he had never been converted. That night he made a total commitment of his life to Jesus Christ, and the Spirit of God began to flow through his life like a mighty river.

(Total commitment to Jesus Christ is the great need of many ministers today. In an article in **Christianity Today** *magazine [December 20, 1974] on the "Great Need for Great Preaching," Dr. James Montgomery Boice noted that 93 percent of the ministerial students of one theological seminary in the U.S. confessed, "I have no devotional life.")*

When the minister returned to his pulpit, there was a change in his preaching and praying. Even though he was a man of great refinement, he began to intersperse expressions of praise—"Hallelujah!" and "Praise the Lord!"—throughout his sermons.

One of the deacons strongly objected to these innovations. He said, "Pastor, don't you realize that still water runs deep?" The pastor did not reply but continued to urge the congregation to seek the fullness of God.

One night during a prayer meeting, the pastor heard a great commotion by the altar. The deacon who had cautioned him against spontaneous outbursts was praising the Lord with a loud voice. His prayer was filled with ecstasy. God had filled him with heaven's joy.

After praying, the deacon's face reflected the glory of God. The pastor could not resist going up to him and saying, "Brother, still water runs deep." The deacon beamed as he replied, "I've not struck still water—I've struck a gusher!"

CAN GOD ANSWER?

The God who stopped the sun on high
(Joshua 10:12,13)
And sent the manna from the sky,
(Exodus 16:4-5)
Laid flat the walls of Jericho
(Joshua 6:20)
And put to flight old Israel's foe,
(Joshua 10:8-10)

Why can't He answer prayer today
(Luke 1:37)
And drive each stormy cloud away
(Matthew 14:31,32)
Who turned the water into wine
(John 2:3-11)
And healed the helpless cripple's spine,
(Luke 13:11-16)

Commands the tempest, "Peace, be still"
(Mark 4:39)
And hungry multitudes doth fill?
(John 6:9-13)
His power is just the same today—
(Hebrews 13:8)
So why not labor, watch and pray?
(Matthew 26:41)

He conquered in the lions' den.
(Daniel 6:16-23)
He brought Lazarus back to life again.
(John 11:38-45)

He heard Elijah's cry for rain
(1 Kings 18:42-45)
    And freed the sufferers from pain.
    (Matthew 8:16,18)

If He could do these wonders then,
    (Exodus 14:21-31)
    Let's prove our mighty God again.
    (Malachi 3:10)
Why can't the God who raised the dead,
    (1 Kings 17:17-22)
    Gave little David Goliath's head,
    (1 Samuel 17:32-51)

Cast out demons with a word,
    (Matthew 8:28-32)
    Yet see the fall of one wee bird,
    (Matthew 10:29)
Do signs and miracles today
    (John 14:12)
    In that same good, old-fashioned way?
    (Acts 5:12-16)

HE CAN! He's just the same today,
    (Ephesians 3:20)
    If we believe God when we pray.
    (Mark 11:23,24)
He's no respecter now of men—
    (James 2:1-9)
HE'LL DO THE SAME AS HE DID THEN!
    —author unknown

Scripture References

1 John 13:27
2 Matthew 26:24
3 Isaiah 37:14
4 See Isaiah 37:38
5 Psalm 34:6
6 James 5:16
7 Mark 10:47
8 Mark 10:48,49

9 Psalm 51:14,15,
     The Amplified Bible
10 See Acts 4:23
11 Acts 4:24
12 Hebrews 5:7
13 Psalm 141:1,2
14 Luke 19:37,38
15 Luke 19:39
16 Luke 19:40

NOTE: These next two chapters are not offered as a treatise on prayer but to encourage you that God will answer your requests. Some of the stories will be amusing, others interesting, and one thing is certain—

THEY REALLY HAPPENED!

CHAPTER FOURTEEN

My First Prayers

It is nothing less than tragic that many people only pray during a crisis. The first prayer I remember hearing in our home was prayed in an electrical storm. The dark clouds, wind and rain created an eerie setting. Suddenly, "Craaack!" A lightning bolt struck nearby. My mother cried out, "O God, help us!" and fled to the basement. This was my introduction to prayer. Later on, my grandmother taught me to pray this child's prayer:

"Now I lay me down to sleep.
I pray the Lord my soul He'll keep.
If I should die before I wake,
I pray the Lord my soul He'll take."

This prayer was more meaningful to me than my mother's and I prayed it occasionally as a boy.

My first prayer

One of my first genuine prayers took place on a Sunday morning when I was about 7 years old. Our family was not serving the Lord. We didn't attend church. My mother was reared as a Catholic and my father was a Protestant (but he wasn't protesting against anything). We were all on our way to hell together.

This particular Sunday morning I was hunting in a field near the road. I noticed the neighbors driving by on their way to church, and I felt a longing in my soul to know God. I prayed hesitantly, "O God, I wish I could know You." Something happened that moment. I was not converted, but I began to talk to God. I knew He had heard my prayer and would answer it someday. Many times after that, while tilling my father's fields or herding his cattle, I would often look up into the heavens at a spectacular cloud formation or at a beautiful sunset and pray, "O God, I wish I could know You."

The Apostle Paul says, *"...the invisible things of him from the creation of the world are clearly seen, being understood by the things that are made, even his eternal power and Godhead; so that they are without excuse: because that when they knew God, they glorified him not as God, neither were thankful; but became vain in their imaginations, and their foolish heart was darkened."*[1] I am thankful that my heart responded to the beauty of God's creation. God had His hand upon me and I knew it.

My second prayer

The second time I began to pray sincerely was when I was dating Connie Brown who later became my wife. By this time, my years of helping Dad on the family farm were coming to an end. I had formed a country-rock dance band and was dreaming of becoming a successful entertainer. I knew the selection of a wife would be very important to my career, so I found myself at a crossroad.

Connie was a beautiful brunette and a good singer. We enjoyed being together. I was very mature for my age, my friends were older and the experience of managing the dance band made me appear much older than I was. Still, when I began to fall in love with Connie, I was just 16. The thought frightened me a bit. What if I married the wrong girl and ruined my life as an entertainer? Keep in mind that I was not a Christian at this time. I did not attend church and I knew nearly nothing about the Bible.

That afternoon, as the tractor hummed along in the field, I realized that only God could tell me if I was right or wrong about marrying Connie. I prayed, "God, if Connie Brown is to be my wife, have her wear the dress I like best when I pick her up tonight." I had never told Connie which of her outfits was my favorite, so the odds of her wearing the dress were less than one in ten. Then I prayed, "God, if she is wearing that dress, I'll know You want me to marry her. If she isn't wearing it, I'll take it as a sign from You that I should break up with her and date someone else."

When I finished my work for the day, I cleaned up and headed for Sisseton as fast as my father's Mercury would fly. My heart was beating faster than ever before as I drove into the Browns' driveway. I'll never forget the moment Connie came bouncing out the door, dressed exactly as I had asked God to have her dressed if He wanted me to marry her. Wow! What a night.

I would not recommend this method of discerning God's will to Christian young people today. The proper way to learn His will is through His Word, the guidance of the Holy Spirit, circumstances which God has brought to bear upon the situation and the advice of fellow Christians. However, asking God for direction in this way became another turning point in my life. I had trusted God with a very important decision. God was working in this matter, too, because several months later Connie invited me to her church. There I heard the Gospel preached with power and later on gave my life to Jesus Christ.

Pray with trust

The Bible says, *"Trust in the Lord with all thine heart; and lean not unto thine own understanding. In all thy ways acknowledge him, and he shall direct thy paths."*[2] Each prayer you pray, trusting God for the answer, will pay off in the years ahead.

I did not accept the Lord right away. After I visited Connie's church and clearly heard the Gospel for the first time, God began to deal with me about my soul. The dance band was making a hit, and I did not want to ruin the chances of its success by becoming a Christian. Also, giving up the band would cost me a lot of money.

One night Connie and I and the band were returning from a dance in Andover, South Dakota. I was exhausted from the strain of our heavy schedule. We had played for a dance in North Dakota the night before. We had performed on two radio shows that day and played for a dance that night. When we headed home at 3:00 a.m., I asked Connie if she would drive. All of the band members including myself were too tired to stay awake.

Just before I drifted off to sleep I took one last look at our schedule and realized that I was going to make a lot of money on the bookings. Just then God spoke to my heart, "Lowell, what will it profit you if you gain the whole world and lose your soul?"

I felt convicted, so I prayed, "God, let me keep my dance band and I will give You part of the money I make. I'll divide the money equally among the churches, and I'll even give some to Connie's church." This was a generous offer because I'd been upset about the sermons I'd heard. The minister kept preaching that I must repent and be born again according to John 3:3.

Be sure you mean what you pray

However, the Holy Spirit continued to urge me to give my life to Christ that moment. Uncomfortable under this pressure, I said, "God, just leave me alone!" He did.

The next thing I remember is Connie screaming and the car flying through the air. I thought, "Oh, no! I'm going to die and I'm not right with God. I have rejected Jesus and my soul is damned." I shouted in terror, "God, give me another chance!" The car rolled over and came to a stop.

We had hit a patch of ice on a curve in the road and gone flying. The car crashed, rolled over and destroyed most of our instruments—but we made it out of the accident alive. When the highway patrolman made out his accident report, he remarked that there weren't any other icy spots in the entire county. There was no doubt in my mind that God had put the ice there to show me the horror of death without Christ.

After the accident, I still refused to serve God, which proves that crisis prayers are prayed by men more concerned about their skins than their sins. Within a few weeks I had a new car and new band instruments and was continuing my career as a country-rock entertainer.

Sometimes God answers before you pray

One morning I was driving back to school after playing for a dance in North Dakota. (Although I grew up in the Sisseton, South

Dakota, area, I attended the high school division of a special agricultural school in Morris, Minnesota, 60 miles east of Sisseton. The school is now the Morris Branch of the University of Minnesota.) As I drove along, admiring my new car, I thought, "Lowell, you're doing well for yourself. Look at all the money you're making."

The Holy Spirit immediately warned me, "Lowell, what will it profit you if you gain the whole world and lose your soul?" I knew God was talking to me again. This time I replied, "God, give me ten years for myself and then I'll serve You. By that time I will be famous." God was displeased with my answer. He pressured me to repent right then. Irritated, I snapped, "God, leave me alone!" He did.

The next thing I remember, the car lurched and I knew I had collided with something. I had apparently fallen asleep while driving against the sun in those early morning hours. In that split second I thought, "I have rejected Jesus again and now I'm going to die." I cried out again, "O God, please give me another chance!"

A moment later I braked my car to a stop. Then I realized I had sideswiped a large truck. The impact demolished the left side of my vehicle. If the car had been just six more inches to the left, I would have been killed. This time I knew for certain that God had spared my life.

I ran back to the truck driver who was sitting behind his steering wheel, stunned. When I got his attention, he mumbled, "I don't know who was with you, kid."

"Why?" I asked.

"As soon as I saw your car on the horizon, *something told me you were going to run into me.* I've been driving along on the edge of this road to get away from you."

God had warned him that I was falling asleep at the wheel and would run into him—even before I prayed. God says, "...*before they call, I will answer; and while they are yet speaking, I will hear.*"[3]

My greatest prayer

My greatest prayer was prayed on Sunday night, April 7, 1957, at 9:30. That was the night I was converted to Jesus Christ. God had been dealing with my heart, and He had spared my life twice. That was also the night I began to comprehend the spiritual battle that had been in progress for my soul.

As Pastor B. C. Heinze preached, my head reeled with doubts: "Should I repent? Why not do it later? How long would my conversion last? Maybe I'd just make a mess of everything by trying to follow Jesus. Maybe I'd make a fool out of God as well as myself." But when the pastor gave the invitation to accept Christ, I almost made up my mind to repent.

Suddenly, I was startled by an unexpected command: "Wait! Don't give your life to God tonight. Think things over for awhile." I realized Satan was attempting to turn me away from Jesus Christ. Alarmed, I rebuked the devil, saying, "Leave me alone!" The disquieting presence of Satan left me, but somehow I still had my doubts about the reality of God.

The Holy Spirit was convicting me and drawing me to Jesus Christ. My soul was sensitive to God. Yet, I had to decide for or against Jesus Christ. My fiancee, Connie, was beside me, praying for me even though she was a backslider herself.

Then I rose and went forward to the second row of pews where I knelt and prayed, "God, if You are really real and if Jesus Christ is Your Son and can really save me so I know it, I want You to save me now." I prayed earnestly, but I seemed to be getting nowhere. Just when I thought I wasn't going to make it, Jesus Christ came into my life.

I was filled with His presence. I felt as though a great burden had been lifted from my shoulders and I had been scrubbed inside and out with Ivory soap. The glory of God came into my life. After ten minutes more, I jumped up and said, "Wait until everyone hears about this!" I HAD BEEN BORN AGAIN!

Pastor Heinze recalls that in the beginning, as I knelt in prayer, I didn't make any progress until I raised my hands and surrendered my entire life to Jesus Christ. The second I prayed, "God, I'll give up my dance band, I'll give up my career as an entertainer, I'll give You all of me," the reality of God exploded within my heart.

The key to my conversion prayer was my willingness to commit my life *totally and irrevocably to God*. UNLESS JESUS CHRIST IS WORTH EVERYTHING, HE IS NOT WORTH ANYTHING; IF HE IS WORTH ANYTHING, HE IS WORTH EVERYTHING. Paul the Apostle says, *"I beseech you therefore, brethren, by the mercies of God, that ye present your bodies a living sacrifice, holy, acceptable unto God, which is your reasonable service."*[4]

My prayer for power

The most dynamic experience, next to my conversion, took place a week after I was converted. My problem was that I lacked the power to be an effective witness for Jesus Christ. As soon as I could, I canceled all of my bookings with the clubs except those for the coming week. I felt it wasn't fair to leave the nightclub owners in the lurch without time to schedule other bands. During this last week with the band, I was discouraged. I wanted to tell people what Christ had done for me, but the people I spoke to were less than impressed.

As I drove home from the second dance engagement, I prayed, "Dear Father, I love You and Jesus Christ, Your Son—but I cannot go on living this Christian life. I don't have the power it takes to be effective. Please help me." The following Sunday, Pastor Heinze and his wife asked Connie and me if we would like to attend a fellowship meeting in Watertown, South Dakota, on Monday night. We said we would.

As we drove the 60 miles to Watertown, Pastor Heinze said, "Lowell, you need to be filled with the Holy Spirit." Evangelist Boneta Rabe, who was with us, agreed. She said, "God's Spirit will give you power to become a witness for Christ." I knew I needed something more from God to be an effective witness.

When the preaching meeting drew to a close that evening, the minister invited Christians to seek the power of God for their individual lives. I think I was the first one to the altar. There I raised my hands and praised God for all He had done for me. Then I asked God to give me more power to be a better witness for Jesus Christ.

Suddenly, it seemed the very gates of heaven swung open and a mighty river of the Spirit of God flowed down upon my soul. Wave after wave of God's power came over me, and I was endued with so much power and glory that I cannot describe it. I began to praise God with a holy utterance, and I felt as though my spirit had been caught up into heaven itself.

After God filled me, I had such power to witness that when dealing with skeptics and mockers I was no longer the victim but the victor! God changed my life so radically that my entire family was influenced to come to Christ within two weeks.

My need to grow in prayer

I still had three nightclub dates to fulfill. The band members gave me a hard time as they rode along in my car for the first three of the last five dances. However, after God filled me with the Holy Spirit, they decided I was "too hot to handle" and drove at their own expense to the last two dance dates.

The Holy Spirit gave me all the power I needed and desired. Only one thing went wrong, and that was my own fault. During the many years I was a nonchristian, my temper was fierce. It was going to trip me up again.

After the last dance, the band members wanted to be paid before they packed the gear. This was not common practice, for they had always been paid after the equipment was loaded. The guys had been needling me throughout the evening, and when they mockingly pressured me to pay them before loading up, I became furious. When that happened, one of the fellows pointed his finger at me and said, "See, you're not a Christian; you're the same old Lowell you've always been."

His comment cut me like a knife. Afterward, I apologized to him, but I had let the Lord down. I think many of those fellows would have been more convinced of Christ in my life if I hadn't become angry that night when they abused me. The Lord says, *"...resist not evil: but whosoever shall smite thee on thy right cheek, turn to him the other also."*[5] Even though you are saved and are experiencing God's power, nonretaliation is the only way

to win your closest friends to Jesus Christ. At
that time I realized my need to grow in
prayer.

Scripture References

1 *Romans 1:20,21*   4 *Romans 12:1*
2 *Proverbs 3:5,6*   5 *Matthew 5:39*
3 *Isaiah 65:24*

CHAPTER FIFTEEN

Growth in Prayer

I'll always remember the first autumn after our family came to Jesus Christ. The weather was beautiful. It gave Dad, my brother, Larry, and me an opportunity to get in some good duck hunting. As boys, we were taught how to hunt and get the most out of the fall season. When the cold wind began to blow out of the northwest, we knew we had only a few good hunting days left. The biggest green-head mallards often stay up north until a big snowstorm drives them south. Within a day or two they would pass through, heading south.

One day a "northwesterner" was blowing up. Dark gray clouds hung low on the horizon and the wind was gusting. Dad, my brother, Larry, and I hooked a grain trailer to Dad's largest tractor and headed for the Peever slough area south of Sisseton. The wind blew furiously and the snow continued to fall. We had taken the tractor instead of the pickup because we didn't want to get stuck in a snowstorm.

When we arrived at the marsh, several miles from the nearest neighbors, the wind was blowing harder and the snowdrifts were getting larger. After an hour, we realized we had driven into the middle of the winter's first full-scale blizzard. Immediately we knew we had to get out of the marsh before the snow got any deeper or we would be trapped in the blizzard and freeze to death before anyone could reach us.

We pushed our way through the snow to the tractor. Dad climbed onto the tractor seat, pressed his foot on the starter, but nothing happened. As usual, the starter did not work. But Dad wasn't worried. He always kept a crank by the tractor motor, and one spin of the crank would get the tractor going again.

The wind was howling and the snow was biting into our faces as Dad yelled, "Lowell, get the crank and give it a turn!" As he adjusted the throttle, he pointed to the place where the crank was carried. I went to pick it up, *but the crank was missing.* Somehow it had been left behind. When I told Dad, his face turned pale. He didn't believe me at first and jumped off the tractor seat to check for himself. Sure enough, the crank was gone. He jumped back on the tractor seat and frantically jammed the starter switch. It was no use; the starter was dead. The seriousness of the howling storm and the miles between us and help chilled us even more than the dropping temperature.

"What should we do?" Dad asked us.

"Let's pray for the starter," I answered.

Dad just smiled a bit because he wasn't sure that God was interested in trivial matters like tractor starters and stranded duck hunters. When he saw that I was serious, he encouraged Larry and me to pray. We raised our hands in the air and prayed that God would activate that starter. After our prayer, Dad tried the starter again, and it worked! It spun the motor over faster than ever before.

We were happy hunters when we headed home.

That night, Dad began to think about what had happened. Unbelief crept into his heart and he thought, "Well, maybe we were just lucky. It's just chance that the starter worked." To satisfy himself, Dad went out to the tractor first thing next morning and tried the starter again. It wouldn't budge. Dad tried the starter off and on for the next three days, but it wouldn't work until he had it repaired. Today he's just as convinced as Larry and I are that God empowered that starter so we wouldn't be trapped in the blizzard. Jesus says, *"If ye shall ask ANYTHING in my name, I will do it."*[1]

This was one of the first times God proved Himself greater than circumstances, but there were to be many more.

The day I claimed a new Greyhound bus

Acquiring adequate transportation facilities for our ministry team has never been easy. During the first years of our ministry,

Connie and I drove a little Rambler station wagon; but later on, when Larry joined us, we purchased a Pontiac sedan with a trailer. As our families grew, the day came when our ministry team required a bus.

Our first bus was literally a disaster. It was called a Flexible Clipper and had been used by the State of California as a mobile office. State officials would drive the bus to the scene of a disaster so that news people would have a place to write and report their stories. The vehicle was equipped with desks and telephones for their use.

Our efforts to convert that mobile office into sleeping quarters were a dismal failure. The heater was inadequate, and there were neither restroom facilities nor air conditioning in the bus.

After five years, we couldn't stand these conditions any longer. Londa and Lisa were growing and could no longer sleep in bed with Connie and me. Larry and Gloria and their first baby slept in the back, and our pianist slept on the front seats. It was tough. In the summer, we roasted. In the winter, snow blew through the cracks in the windows and drifted onto our beds.

One day we drove by Pembina, North Dakota, where the Greyhound Bus Company assembles new Scenicruisers. The bus bodies are built in Winnipeg, Manitoba, and shipped on flat-bed trucks to Pembina (on the U.S.-Canadian border) where the motors and running gear are assembled.

The company had just completed a new model of a 40-foot Scenicruiser. It was beautiful. It had every feature we needed in a bus—heating, air conditioning, restroom facilities and room to build bunks or bedrooms. Besides, it had enough storage area to carry our equipment.

As I stood beside the towering $72,000 Scenicruiser, I was flat broke. Jokingly I tell friends I didn't have enough money to buy birdseed for a cuckoo clock. I knew, despite the financial barrier, God was able to provide a bus like this for our ministry. I definitely felt He wanted our children to grow up with access to a restroom.

We were nearly always on the lookout for a flying red horse, which used to be the insignia of Mobil Oil Company gas stations. Sometimes the children used a special plastic container (The team called it a honey bucket) and forgot to put it away. In the morning, I'd jump out of bed and be shocked by an ice-cold feeling on my foot. I'd stepped into the honey bucket!

The more I thought about God's goodness and our need for a Scenicruiser, the more I was convinced that God wanted us to have one. So I placed both of my hands on the side of that bus and prayed, "Dear Father, I believe You want our children to have a comfortable home. I claim this bus for Your ministry, for Your glory. In Jesus' name, amen."

Instantly faith filled my heart and God showed me a plan to raise the funds to buy this new vehicle. The first thing He instructed me to do was park our old puddle-jumper behind the beautiful new Scenicruiser and send a photo to all of our partners. The photo would tell the story. Then He instructed me to set up a tour of places where pastors and friends who believed in our ministry would allow me to present the need.

Within a few months God provided the entire $72,000. When we picked up the bus in Columbus, Ohio, where it had been out-fitted to our specifications, it was paid for in full!

Praise God! I will never forget the thrill of sitting down and blowing the air horn for the first time. It was the trumpet sound of victory! This bus has traveled a million miles and is still carrying the Lundstroms from crusade to crusade. Since we purchased this bus, the Lord has provided two more new buses through His faithfulness and the partnership of our friends.

This is the lesson we learned that will help you. If you have a great need and have been faithful to the Lord with what He has given you, if you are convinced that He wants to provide you with something better and more appropriate for your present needs, take a step of faith! Claim what you need in Jesus' name. God will work a miracle for you. Chances are that God will give you a plan just as He did for us, and you will be re-joicing because of His provision. Jesus says, *"...Have faith in God. For verily I say unto you, That whosoever shall SAY unto this mountain, Be thou removed, and be thou cast into the sea;*

*and shall not doubt in his heart, but shall believe
that those things which he SAITH shall come to
pass; he shall have whatsoever he SAITH. Therefore I say unto you, What things soever ye desire,
when ye pray, believe that ye receive them, and ye
shall have them.''*[2]

Whatever you confess, you will possess.
Pray in faith, claiming God's promise to
meet your need. YOU CAN PRAY WITH
POWER AND GET RESULTS.

*The night God
healed my sinuses*

One of the physical drawbacks I had as an
entertainer, prior to my conversion, was the
weakness in my sinus passages. I was constantly fighting infections. Some days I
would fill as many as ten large handker-
chiefs with mucus.

One Sunday evening, about a month after
I accepted the Lord, I realized how foolish I
was to allow my infected sinuses to trouble
me. After all, God is great and powerful, and
He promises to heal us if we ask Him to.

During the "after service," I went forward and asked the pastor to anoint me with oil. As soon as he prayed, I felt the blockage break open. I could breathe easily through my nose for the first time in years. I went over to a deacon, Carl Johnson (who is my wife's uncle), and said, "Listen—I'll blow air through my nose to show you how God has healed me!" I had reason to rejoice because this answer to prayer made my ministry much easier. *My faith was growing.*

I believe that God heals people today because I have been healed many times. Some may deny that miracles happen today, but I read once that people seldom believe in miracles until they need one. James asks, *"Is any sick among you? Let him call for the elders of the church; and let them pray over him, anointing him with oil in the name of the Lord; and the prayer of faith shall save the sick, and the Lord shall raise him up...."*[3]

I hope my experiences in prayer will encourage you to seek God for your need.

What is your need?

Healing, money, a better house or car, the salvation of a loved one, or a fresh filling of the Holy Spirit? Whatever your need is, remember that you have the privilege of prayer in Jesus Christ. Whatever you ask in Jesus' name, believing, God has promised to do.

So pray right now. CONFESS WHAT YOU WANT TO POSSESS. Speak up and claim whatever you need from God, for what you SAY is what you GET!

Scripture References

1 *John 14:14*   3 *James 5:14,15*
2 *Mark 11:22-24*

CHAPTER SIXTEEN

Living in the Spirit of Prayer

South Dakota gets very cold in the winter, sometimes ⁻30°F with a wind-chill factor as low as ⁻60°F. Without proper precautions in this frigid weather, starting a car engine is almost impossible—the oil is so thick that the pistons can barely move. Most Dakotans solve the problem by hooking an electric headbolt heater to the engine block. This device heats the motor constantly so the engine is ready to start.

With the "sin-chill" factor as low as it is in the world today, we need to keep our hearts hot for God. The Apostle Paul says that we should be "...*continuing instant in prayer*...."[1] According to the Apostle Luke, Jesus Christ

Himself says that *"...men ought always to pray."*[2] The Lord commands, *"...pray always, that ye may be accounted worthy...to stand before the Son of man."*[3]

A key to praying with power is to live in a spirit of prayer. You must learn to be sensitive to the Holy Spirit's promptings. If you practice constant communion with God, you won't need to pump up your soul when you need to pray for a miracle.

The turbines of the Grand Coulee Dam are powered by the controlled flow of water from the Franklin D. Roosevelt Lake. Whenever more power needs to be generated, the dam's gigantic gates open to send water rushing through the turbines. If the U.S. Bureau of Reclamation hadn't designed and constructed the reservoir lake out of the waters of the Columbia River, the river's water level could be too low to produce sufficient power in a crisis.

You need to continually store God's power in your mind and heart through prayer—while you work, play, sleep, eat, *etc.* If you think that you cannot pray and work at the same time, you're wrong. People work and chew gum, people work and whistle, people work and visit with a co-worker—then why not work and talk to God? Most of your body functions utilize less than ten percent of your brain capacity. Learn to pray constantly.

I try to maintain a spirit of prayer all day and all night regardless of what I am doing

● I pray before I get out of bed in the morning. As soon as I awaken, I roll over on my stomach, place my head in my hands and praise the Lord for what He has done and is going to do. Sometimes I fall back to sleep, but I don't get uptight over this because this is not the time when I formally make petitions to God in prayer. In these early morning moments I tell God how much I love Him just as a child dozing in his father's arms murmurs contentedly, ''I love you, Daddy.''

In fact, if you read God's Word and fall asleep in an attitude of prayer, your subconscious mind will pray and review God's promises while you sleep. David declared, *"...my mouth shall praise thee* [O God] *with joyful lips: when I remember thee upon my bed, and meditate on thee in the night watches."*[4]

● Then I pray while taking my morning shower. I praise God and express my love to Him with my words. As I shave, I'll pray, "Lord, bless that guy who's looking at me in the mirror. Without Your blessing, he's as dead as a stick."

● Before, during and after breakfast, I pray and read the Bible or a good Christian growth book, and I share thoughts from the reading selection with whoever is present.

● I pray while I drive around town or down some highway. During a city-wide crusade, my days are often booked up with speaking engagements and television, radio and newspaper interviews. On these occasions, either a crusade director or publicity chairman drives while I read God's Word. We pray before we arrive at the location of my speaking engagement. Then if I feel a heavy spirit of oppression hanging over the gathering, a satanic conflict, I excuse myself and go to a janitor's closet, furnace room or men's room. There I plead the blood of Jesus over the meeting and pray through to liberty. I have to "bind the strong man," or he will bind me.

● I pray while driving through city traffic. Each red light becomes a prayer point. If I were you, I would try to purchase an inexpensive cassette tape player for the car (Some models cost about $39) and plug it into the cigarette lighter. Then you could play sermon tapes and Scripture readings to charge your soul with God's Word.

You may think that putting so much time and effort into prayer is extreme. But it isn't, really. John Wesley divided his life into five-minute periods of time and endeavored to make each period count for God.

I'll give you one extra bit of advice. Learning how to pray with your eyes open and without moving your lips helps to keep nearby drivers and pedestrians from thinking that you've lost your mind. I forgot my own advice one time at Chicago's O'Hare Airport. I'd just gone to a men's room, and I thought it was empty. As I washed my hands, I shouted, "O God, I love You!"

Then out of the corner of my eye I noticed a man tiptoeing past me to the door. He had a frightened look on his face.

● I pray while waiting on the telephone—while the operator looks for a number and while waiting for someone to answer my phone call.

● I pray before the evening meeting. In addition to the time I've spent in prayer throughout the day, I usually spend between 30 and 60 minutes with God before I preach. Prayer helps to fine-tune my spirit to God's perfect will.

Thomas Goodwin, a Puritan, wrote, "The Holy Spirit who is the intercessor within us, and who searches the deep things of God, doth offer, prompt, and suggest to us in our prayers these very things that are in God's heart, to grant the thing we desire of Him, so as it often comes to pass that a poor creature is carried on to speak God's very heart to Himself, and then God cannot, nor doth deny..." the request we make to Him.

● I pray while I read the Bible. Jesus says, *"Blessed are they which do hunger and thirst after righteousness: for they shall be filled."*[5]

John Bunyan tells how Satan tried to tear the Word of God from his heart: "Satan would labor to pull the promise from me, telling me that Christ did not mean me in John 6:37. **(In this reference, Jesus says,** *"All that the Father giveth me shall come to me: and him that cometh to me I will in no wise cast out."*—**Lowell)** He pulled, and I pulled. But God be praised, I got the better of him."

Your key to praying with power is to turn your heart into a 24-hour prayer room. "True prayer," writes Samuel M. Zwemer, "is God the Holy Spirit talking to God the Father in the name of God the Son, and the believer's heart is the prayer room."

The Apostle Paul says, *"Let this mind be in you, which was also in Christ Jesus...."*[6] He also says, *"...Walk in the Spirit...."*[7] When your heart becomes a 24-hour-a-day prayer room, you will begin to pray with greater power than you have ever known.

When you pray in the Spirit, you are not praying from earth to heaven, you are actually praying from your exalted position at the right hand of God. Paul says that God has made you spiritually alive in Christ and given you a place in heaven.[8]

You are not begging a sovereign for a handout. By faith, you are seated with Jesus Christ upon His throne! As Paul Billheimer says, "We are co-crucified with Christ; we are co-raised with Christ; we are co-exalted with Christ; and we are *co-seated with Christ*."

If you think that you are only one of four billion people trying to project your prayers across the vast regions of space to an unknown god who may or may not answer, you will be defeated in prayer. But if by faith you realize that through Jesus Christ you have been exalted to the Father's right hand and that you have the power of attorney to pray in Jesus' name, *you are on the road to victory*. As a born-again believer, this realization will fill your prayers with faith and you will shake the world!

Your position of privilege in prayer

Many people immigrated to the United States in the 1800s. One day a man who decided to find his fortune in the new country pooled his life savings and purchased a ticket on an oceanliner bound for America.

When he set out, he was so broke that he couldn't afford to eat at the ship's cafeteria, so he went without food for two weeks. Then one night the ship was caught in a violent storm, and the immigrant became seasick. Afterward, he was hungrier than ever.

Realizing that he would die if he didn't get some food to eat, he stumbled down to the cafeteria and ate as much food as he could hold. He thought, "It's better to be thrown into jail for not paying the bill than to starve!"

Facing up to the worst that could happen, he asked the waiter for the bill. But the waiter exclaimed, "Why, there isn't any charge! Meals are included in the price of your ticket!" Through ignorance, the immigrant had nearly starved to death for nothing.

Remember what Jesus promised you when you boarded His grand old Gospel ship, *The Church*: "...*Whatsoever ye shall ask the Father in my name, HE WILL GIVE IT TO YOU. ...ASK, AND YE SHALL RECEIVE, THAT YOUR JOY MAY BE FULL.*"[9]

The Apostle John says, *"Beloved, I wish above all things that thou mayest prosper and be in health, even as thy soul prospereth."*[10] Don't read this book on prayer and lay it aside. Memorize the promises and share them with your friends. Read the helpful passages in prayer meetings. Then pass this book on to a friend. The whole world needs to know that Jesus Christ has paid the ticket price to God's blessings in full. His precious blood has given us access to God the Father and all the treasures of heaven! Hallelujah!

God says, *"...YE SHALL SEEK ME, AND FIND ME, WHEN YE SHALL SEARCH FOR ME WITH ALL YOUR HEART."*[11]

Scripture References

1 *Romans 12:12*

2 *Luke 18:1*

3 *Luke 21:36*

4 *Psalm 63:5,6*

5 *Matthew 5:6*

6 *Philippians 2:5*

7 *Galatians 5:16*

8 *See Ephesians 2:5,6*

9 *John 16:23,24*

10 *3 John, verse 2*

11 *Jeremiah 29:13*